Coming

Coming All the Way Home

*Memoir of an Assault
Helicopter Aircraft Commander
in Vietnam*

FRED MCCARTHY

McFarland & Company, Inc., Publishers
Jefferson, North Carolina

All photographs courtesy Bill Schmidt unless otherwise noted.
All poems by Fred McCarthy
"A Date with an Old Girlfriend" (in Chapter 20) originally appeared in *The VHPA Aviator* (May–June 2020) and "A Headstone for Thousands," by Tom Kirk (also in Chapter 20), originally appeared in *The VHPA Aviator* (July–August 2018). Both are used by permission.

Frontispiece: This is where the crew chief and door gunner sat when we took off or landed. They would crawl out on the pylon and shoot covering fire under the helicopter as we banked hard and broke from a gun or rocket run. The only thing holding them from falling was a webbed "monkey strap." They hand-held and fired a 30-caliber machine gun (author photo).

LIBRARY OF CONGRESS CATALOGUING-IN-PUBLICATION DATA

Names: McCarthy, Fred, 1946– author.
Title: Coming all the way home : memoir of an assault helicopter aircraft commander in Vietnam / Fred McCarthy.
Other titles: Memoir of an assault helicopter aircraft commander in Vietnam
Description: Jefferson, North Carolina : McFarland & Company, Inc., Publishers, 2021 | Includes bibliographical references and index.
Identifiers: LCCN 2021022108 | ISBN 9781476684703 (paperback : acid free paper) ∞
    ISBN 9781476643571 (ebook)
Subjects: LCSH: McCarthy, Fred, 1946- | United States. Army. Assault Helicopter Company, 175th—Biography. | Helicopter pilots—United States—Biography. | Helicopter pilots—Vietnam—Biography. | United States. Army—Officers—Biography. | Vietnam War, 1961-1975—Aerial operations, American. | Vietnam War, 1961-1975—Personal narratives, American. | BISAC: HISTORY / Military / Vietnam War
Classification: LCC DS558.8 .M319 2021 | DDC 959.704/34092 [B]—dc23
LC record available at https://lccn.loc.gov/2021022108

BRITISH LIBRARY CATALOGUING DATA ARE AVAILABLE

ISBN (print) 978-1-4766-8470-3
ISBN (ebook) 978-1-4766-4357-1

Front cover: *Guns Up* (Joe Kline, Aviation Artist)

Printed in the United States of America

McFarland & Company, Inc., Publishers
Box 611, Jefferson, North Carolina 28640
www.mcfarlandpub.com

This book is dedicated to the memory of 30 flight crewmembers who made the ultimate sacrifice for their country, serving with the U.S. Army's 121st Assault Helicopter Company at Soc Trang, in the Mekong Delta IV Corps area, or Da Nang in I Corps during the Vietnam War. And to those who came home but left an important part of who they were in Vietnam.

The Rice Fields Are Burning

It's early in the new year and the rice fields are burning. My heart finds a certain yearning to be among friends; sharing the things we used to share, caring the way we used to care.

And yet the experience of being here of burning away the child in me, should strengthen the soil that I might grow with a little bit more maturity

Table of Contents

Acknowledgments

Family Appreciation

My deepest appreciation to my understanding and supportive wife, Shannon; two successful risk-taking sons, Mike and Pat; lovely daughters-in-law, Megan and Bethany; and very special grandchildren, Milo, Lizah, and Rowen, for putting up with me and my quirky behavior and for loving me anyway through it all.

Veteran Appreciation

Jim Lucking—Jim's personal friendship and mentoring was instrumental in my completion of flight school, in my success as a slick pilot with the Tigers, and in my becoming an aircraft commander in B model gunships with the Vikings of the 121st Assault Helicopter Company. We were in the best company in the U.S. Army, the world-famous Soc Trang Tigers, based in Soc Trang, Republic of Vietnam, during 1967 and 1968. A part of him has been with me all of my life in the many leadership roles I have been privileged to hold as a civilian. I can't thank him enough for the difference he made in the quality of my life.

Paul Woodby—Paul came to the 121st Assault Helicopter Company as an experienced infantry soldier and pathfinder and took on the challenging role of becoming a door gunner with the Vikings. Door gunners hung out the side of a Huey on a "monkey strap" and fired their machine guns under the aircraft as it broke from a gun or rocket run. It was a very dangerous job, and he did it with skill, courage, and dedication to the mission. We shared the experience of a night engine failure and an autorotation in a fully loaded Viking B model Huey gunship on October 18, 1968. After we were evacuated by a Dustoff medevac helicopter, the aircraft was destroyed by the Viet Cong. We consider ourselves brothers of a different mother for life.

Writing, Editing and Publishing Appreciation

Writing this book has been a fulfillment of a life-long dream to recount one of the most memorable adventures of my life. I appreciate the inspiration and technical assistance that was so readily available from some very special people I was fortunate to meet along the way.

I would like to thank the following members of the Vicious Writers' Circle on Whidbey Island for their insightful comments at a time when the project needed direction and honest critique: Dan Pedersen, Chris Spencer, JoAnn Kane, Candace Allen, Dave Anderson, and Regina Hugo.

I would like to thank Elizabeth (Beth) Hall for her considerable editing skills and suggestions. She mentored me through a number of substantial revisions and reorganizations of this book.

I would also like to thank Dylan Lightfoot, editor at McFarland, for his editing suggestions and input on revision.

Military Terminology

AC—aircraft commander—pilot in command—sits in the right seat
ARVN—Army of the Republic of Vietnam—South Vietnamese soldiers
Ballistic helmet—theoretically capable of deflecting some bullets
Bullet bouncer—bulletproof Kevlar plate to protect the chest
C-rations—1200-calorie meal in a can for use in the field
Collective—control that adds or takes out pitch in the rotor blades
Combat assault—an operation involving slicks and gunships and a command and control helicopter to airlift troops into a landing zone
CW2—Chief Warrant Officer 2 (Levels WO1, CW2, CW3, CW4)
Cyclic—control stick that comes up between the legs of the pilot for directional control of the aircraft
Deuce and a half—a 2.5-ton truck for carrying supplies or soldiers
EGT–Exhaust Gas Temperature—a temperature gauge of the helicopter's turbine engine exhaust
FNG—F---ing New Guy
.45—Colt .45 standard issue Army sidearm (pistol)
Hooches—thatched roof and sides, houses, or storage sheds sometimes containing weapons and ammunition; also the barracks where we lived
KIA—killed in action
Klick—kilometer—metric measurement =.6214 of a mile—standard for stating distance to the target or objective in the military, etc.
LZ—landing zone
M60s—flexible mounted machine guns fed by linked bullets
Mic—microphone on flight helmet
Monkey strap—webbed strap attaching crewmember to the helicopter when climbing out on the rocket pods to fire their weapons
P38—can opener for opening C-ration cans of food
Pacs—passengers—armed troops in a combat assault
POL—refueling area (Petroleum, Oil, Lubricants)

Pull pitch—pulling up on the collective control that adds pitch in the
   blades and causes the helicopter to go up or down
PZ–pick-up zone—where infantry troops are loaded for a mission
RP—reporting point
Short final—final approach to landing
Sit rep—situation report—report of what's happening in an operation
Slicks—troop transport helicopters as opposed to gunships
SOP—Standard Operating Procedure
TAC–Tactical Officer supervises Warrant Officer Candidates
.38—police standard issue pistol issued to pilots to replace the .45
Trim resistance—a control to set the cyclic in a climb. If the pilot lets go of
   this control the aircraft will climb rather than nose over
V of three—three helicopters flying in a v formation

Preface

This is a true story of a 21-year-old's one-year transition from monastic life in a seminary to a U.S. Army helicopter gunship aircraft commander in the Vietnam War. He is motivated by a family tradition of combat service, a strong sense of patriotism, a love for aviation, and a desire for adventure. He gets far more than he bargained for. He shares some exciting flying missions, reflects on the nature of being a combat pilot, and processes the experience through his poetry, letters home, and reflective analysis. He takes the reader through the history and morality of this war and the role of the combat soldier. This is partially a war story, but more than that, it straps readers into the armored seat in the cockpit of a helicopter gunship and lets them have a first-person experience of how this adventure defined a young man's life. His hope in writing this memoir is to share with others the intensely personal legacy of war that comes with the experience. Writing the book involved 50 years of discernment, reading, and study. In some small way he hopes to help the reader understand a war experience and perhaps help other Vietnam veterans and their families also come all the way home.

1

Baptism by Fire

I am leaning into the bulletproof armored panel with my left shoulder. Resting on my lap is a ¾-inch bullet bouncer that extends up to my neck to stop bullets that come through the windscreen. The fireproof gloves are pulled tightly over my fingers, and I glance at the time on my watch. The belt for my side arm is rotated so that my .45 is between my legs to protect the family jewels. I turn the knob and pull the dark visor of the ballistic helmet down over my face to protect my eyes. I'm as ready as I can be for my first mission as a gunship pilot.

Above my head is a gun sight for firing twin M60 machine guns, mounted on flexible mounts, two on each side of the aircraft. Our door gunner and crew chief rest their feet on the machine gun pylons on the outside of the cabin area. The crewmembers are locked and loaded and ready to climb out onto the pylons, secured only by a monkey strap, to shoot under and behind the aircraft as we break from our gun and rocket runs. Looking over the barrels of their handheld machine guns, they scan the mangroves and canals below looking for movement and any signs of black-clad Viet Cong.

The cockpit is a uniquely surrealistic world. There are 100 switches, gauges, and breakers, etc., that feel like they are an extension of our extremities. After many hours in the cockpit we can tell their location by feel. We let down five klicks (kilometers) out of the landing zone and are hauling ass, balls to the wall, at treetop level, pushing 90 knots over a mangrove tree line leading up to the area of operation. The rotor blades are whop-whopping in familiar Huey-style syncopation at this airspeed, and the whole damn aircraft is shaking as the advancing rotors claw the air. I am the co-pilot in the lead gunship.

The aircraft commander is talking on the radio to Tiger Six in the command and control ship up above us at 1,000 feet, in what we call the nosebleed section of the theater, circling the area. The commander is asking him for a sitrep and what it looks like down at treetop level where the operation is about to unfold. My job is to scan the instruments, have my fingers on the trigger of the M60s, call out anything I see to the aircraft commander, and be ready to take the controls if necessary. We are flying a light gun team today consisting of two gunships.

I activate the armament as we descend from altitude. I turn on the firing systems for both of us up front on the center console. "Guns and rockets are hot," I say over the intercom for the benefit of the crew, part of our standard operating procedure.

The aircraft commander in the right seat controls the firing of rockets with a button on his cyclic control, and he also fires the flex guns if necessary (if the co-pilot is unable) by toggling a switch on the center console. I am in the left seat with my right hand on the gunsight trigger. I pull it down in front of me and look out over the glass reticle that is the gunsight. Every action has a contingency procedure and a back-up plan. The aircraft commander cranks down the friction on the collective to set the power for low-level flight and sets the trim on the cyclic stick in a climb. The rationale is if one or both of us up front gets shot, our aircraft will climb up when the cyclic is released, rather than nose over and take out the rest of the crew.

The aircraft commander holds forward pressure on the cyclic pushing against the trim resistance. The crew feels one with the tired old B model Huey. The instruments are alive, the gauges are in the green, we are loaded for bear, and we settle into the shake, rattle and roll rhythm of a helicopter combat assault mission.

We are low-leveling just above the treetops, following a line of scraggly nipa palms that hide a canal and lead to the landing zone. We S turn at 85 knots along the tops of the jungle canopy and pop up and over a line of trees and drop down into the open area of the LZ. We are trying to draw fire and get the Viet Cong to shoot at us so that we can return fire and clear the way for the incoming slicks. Everyone in the aircraft is on heightened alert looking for Cong in the landing zone, suspicious structures, explosives, or hidden enemy soldiers. We know that sometimes the VC hide caches of explosives in stacks of straw, huts, or dense foliage, so we shoot a few rockets into them to see if we can hit pay dirt. It's like playing the lottery hoping for a jackpot.

The landing zone is about a klick in diameter, with huts and other structures, and lots of hidden places for Viet Cong to hide. Ahead I see what appears to me to be a man in black pajamas crouching beside a bush with a weapon. Before I know it, we are over him. He raises an AK-47 and unloads on us. Pop pop pop pop pop. We break right and head for the tree line.

The AC keys the mic and tells our wingman in a low and controlled matter-of-fact voice, "21 receiving light automatic weapons fire and breaking right." We fly towards the tree line, turn over it, and parallel the LZ at treetop level. I crane my neck to look back over my shoulder to see if I can pinpoint the enemy and his location.

The AC scans the instruments and then the operational area side to side and says to me, "What the hell were you doing back there? We don't have the time to figure out whether a gook in black pajamas with a weapon is our friend or not. Obviously that guy was not. We're coming around and you better grease him if he is still there." We came around, he was, and I did.

The aircraft commander calls our wingman: "22, this is 21. We are confirming one KIA. Let's prep this LZ for the slicks." The door gunner and crew chief start calling out targets from their respective sides of the helicopter and firing at the same time. The sound is deafening. Spent bullet casings bounce around the cabin. I feel something hot on my neck, and it turns out to be a few spent casings from the crew's machine guns, their way to welcome me to my first gunship mission. We shoot into hooches and tree lines and fire a couple of rockets into haystacks. Our heads are on swivels, my heart is in my throat, and we are trying to figure out whether this place is going to blow up in our face when the transports descend down into the landing zone. None of the hooches or haystacks produces a secondary explosion. We separate from our wingman, widen our track, break off, and now fly two racetrack patterns 180 degrees out of sync with each other over the tree lines on either side of the landing zone. We space our aircraft out in an orchestrated dance by going a little wider in the turn so that when one gunship is rolling in, the other is turning away on the backside of the oval pattern. These are our tactics that we have down like clockwork.

After four of these circuits, we fly in low, down the middle of LZ Alpha in the lead gunship. Our wingman is following in a crazy zigzag pattern about three football fields behind us. The AC tells the crew chief to get ready to pop smoke. We come in even lower over the rice paddy, bobbing and weaving like a saddle bronc rider in a rodeo, and on command the crew chief pulls the pin and throws out a grenade-sized canister. It hits the ground, tumbles, and erupts with red smoke that blows to the east over the landing zone.

Tiger Lead and the eight other slicks at reporting point 5 now have the directional wind information they need and a targeted landing spot for the lead aircraft in the formation. The D model transports have formed up into Vs of three, with nine total slicks, each with eight ARVN soldiers in the formation, and they leave their circling pattern on a westerly heading of 270 degrees for the LZ. "Viking 21, this is Tiger Lead departing RP5, have the red smoke." The formation of slicks begins their descent. The trajectory looks good. They are now about two klicks out. The formation is tight, the rotors almost overlapping. The slick drivers have nailed down their sight pictures and picked spots on the aircraft they are referencing, and the crews are getting psyched for their touchdown in the landing zone. The aerial dance of the formation manifests itself in a semi-chaotic movement up and down in the hot and humid 100-degree blast furnace of the dry season in the Mekong Delta. Every crewmember on each transport ship is feeling an increased sense of adrenaline and awareness. The crew chief and door gunner on each slick are hunched over their swivel mounted M60s, looking for VC and ready to fire.

Things are quiet. Too quiet. The last part of our final approach to touchdown, when the shit starts hitting the fan. As Tiger Lead touches down, the radios come alive with calls of "receiving fire, taking hits, from the tree line to the north." We hear the sound of weapons firing above the static of the slicks' radios when the aircraft commanders key their mics: "Viking 21, this is Tiger 6, what is going on down there? Are you taking any fire?"

"Roger that, sir, we are," responds CW2 Peterson in a low-pitched drawl. Popping sounds in the background accompany each radio call.

"Well, how bad is it?"

"Wait one, sir!" is the response.

The next transmission, in another deep, low-pitched voice, comes from Peterson: "Tiger Lead, this is Viking 21, understand, receiving fire from the north tree line. The Vikings are on it. Call out the fire, dump your pacs, and get the hell out of there."

The lead transport aircraft begins touching down in the rice paddy. In rapid succession, each ship starts to flare as the formation bleeds off airspeed and slows for touchdown. The formation breaks apart as each aircraft commander moves to an open area away from obstacles like dikes and small palms and picks his own best spot for touchdown. The troops jump out of the Hueys and disappear into the tall reeds and rice paddies. Each V of three is on the ground for only a few seconds. The rotors are spinning, muddy rice paddy water is spraying up in the air, partially obscuring the windscreen, and the ARVNs are bent over holding on to their helmets and weapons and making for cover. Over the mic come the words "Tiger Lead, pulling pitch," signaling that the pacs are out of the lead ship. Tiger Lead has waited a few seconds on the ground for each ship to offload, and then they are departing the landing zone.

The crew chiefs and door gunners in the slicks have been pushing the soldiers of the Army of the Republic of Vietnam (ARVN) off and then shooting over their heads into the tree line. Each set of three slicks pulls pitch, angles apart slightly from the others, and accelerates forward with noses down and airspeed building fast, having jettisoned the weight of the infantry cargo. On the way out, there are calls of "Tiger 2, taking fire" and "Tiger 5 took a hit from the north tree line." The last set of three helicopters is off, and the aircraft climb rapidly in a left turn to an altitude of 1,000 feet.

On the way up to altitude, they join in another formation for the trip back to the pick-up zone (PZ) for another load. No reports of "going down" are heard, and we in the guns start breathing again.

Sporadic shots are taken at the last couple of slicks, particularly the last ship, as it departs the LZ, and the first of five insertions comes to closure for the slick drivers. As the "trail" slick (last in formation) climbs to altitude, the gunships are firing into the tree lines above the ARVN troops, and they stay on station and make a few more racetrack runs around the LZ.

"Tiger 6, Viking 21."

"21, this is 6. Go ahead."

"Sir, the insertion is completed. We are covering the pacs into the tree lines, light fire in the LZ, one KIA."

We are unloading on the areas where the fire was reported, multiple hooches and suspect areas, and following the inserted troops out of the rice paddies and into the tree lines. After about 15 minutes of overflying the area, the guns low-level out of the operational area and climb up and away from the landing zone and out over the rice paddies to 1,000 feet for the trip back to Can Tho for refueling and rearming. The whole operation in the landing zone from prep to drop-off takes about 30 minutes.

Four more combat assaults go in to LZ Alpha on this day. The slicks are standing by at a staging field in between runs. It's just a road out in the middle of nowhere along the crest of a dike line where they are picking up their ARVN infantry soldiers. Two times during the afternoon the slicks come in formation into Can Tho and refuel. The gunships fly on in to Can Tho after each insertion and hover to the POL area for refueling/rearming on the airfield, and the crew chiefs begin the process of fueling up the thirsty gunships while the door gunners load up metal boxes of machine gun ammunition. The aircraft commander walks back to check in with his wingman, and I start pulling the rockets out of the storage area, cranking on the warheads, and filling the seven tubes on each side with the 2.75-inch rockets left over from World War II. I am saying a silent Hail Mary each time I place the rocket body on my knee and crank on the warhead before loading it in a tube and moving the firing striker to contact ass-end of each rocket, secretly hoping that one doesn't blow up in my face.

The smell of jet fuel and gunpowder is intoxicating, and it is hotter than hell this time of the year. We leave our sweat-stained jungle fatigue shirts draped on the mesh seats to dry and wear just the black T-shirts that are a distinct identifying mark of the Vikings from the 121st Assault Helicopter Company out of Soc Trang.

There are also other gunships refueling and rearming today. The Mavericks of the 175th Assault Helicopter Company out of Vinh Long are

turning around their C model fire teams as well. Their pilots wear red neck-
erchiefs tied around their necks, identifying them as the cowboys they are.
They are working the war nearby. We are glad we fly these tacked together
and tired old B models because they are lighter and more maneuverable
than the newer C models and we can fly them right on the treetops and
do steep banked turns without falling out of the sky. The C model, with its
touted 540-rotor system, unloads in a turn and loses altitude, so the Mavericks fly their missions at about 300 feet, where you are, from our point of
view, a sitting duck.

The next four assaults we are involved in that day result in return trips
to LZ Alpha with only sporadic and isolated gunfire. It's the same song,
same dance, next verse, sometimes louder, and sometimes a whole lot
worse. The routines of refueling, rearming, and waiting in between lifts are
repeated throughout the day. After the fifth operation, the Viking gun team
heads east for home towards our Delta base at Soc Trang.

Five miles out, CW2 Peterson keys the mic: "Soc Trang Tower, this is
Viking 21. Flight of two Vikings five miles west of Soc Trang for landing."

"Viking 21, this is Soc Trang Tower, cleared to land." The gunship team
starts descending in a long base leg and then turns right on a one-mile final.

"OK, you've got the controls. Take her in and land her," Pete says casually to me.

I answer: "Roger that, I've got the controls." With my hands taking
over the cyclic and collective and my feet on the pedals, I line the gunship up on final approach. In the back of my mind, I know that we have just
refueled and rearmed at Can Tho and the aircraft is heavy and will be difficult to slow down, but if I flare it out too abruptly it may not have enough
lift to hover down the runway. The wingman is right behind me. The process
of landing this aircraft is a tense balancing act especially for a first-timer.

We come in over the concertina wire and bunkers at the north end of
the runway at about 80 knots and start a flare. The Viking parking revetments are about one-fourth of the way down the runway. The damn aircraft
is not slowing down. It floats and floats and floats about three feet above the
runway, and then we sail on past the revetments for parking. I look over at
Pete as if to say, "Shall we turn around and hover back to the parking revetment?" and he says, "Go around!"

I'm thinking, "Man, the guys in the back end and the wing ship are
wondering what the hell is going on up here." So I nose the helicopter over
and climb out straight ahead and look to Pete as if to say, "What next?" and
he says, "Do it again" and keys the mic to acknowledge: "Tower, 21 is on the
go. Close traffic for another approach."

"21 is cleared as requested!" is the tower's response. Meanwhile the
wingman behind us hovers over into their sandbagged revetment. We turn

crosswind and downwind and set up for a quarter-mile final to the revetment area. This time I come over the wire at 70 knots and start to flare and
sail on by the revetments again.

"One more time," Pete says.

I am dying and sweating bullets and wondering if I can get this sucker
down. It doesn't help that I can sense the distain of the crew in the back end
for having to turn this return trip into basic landing practice for a new gunship co-pilot on a long hot day. The third time I start slowing earlier and
bring the gunship to a one-foot hover over the runway. We stop even with
the revetment, turn in and hover over and slide the aircraft into position
between the metal 50-gallon drums around the sandbagged revetment. I
lower the collective for a one-two bounce of the skids on the ground and
a collective sigh of relief from the crew. I roll off the throttle, being certain
that the collective is in the full down position and my feet are set on the
pedals so the tail doesn't rotate into the side of the revetment.

We go through the engine shutdown procedure. It is dead silent in the
cockpit as the aircraft commander fills out the maintenance record book. I
am ready to apologize for my miserable display of airmanship. "We'll talk
about it later," says Pete. The crew are quite enjoying my uncomfortable
feelings as they tie down the rotor blades. The crew chief, a crusty old salt,
says, "Way to go, babysan." I am aware that I've always looked young for my
age and look about 16 years old when I am 21. I wonder if I am going to get
the heave-ho for this miserable display of questionable flying skills, if this
first gunship mission was in fact my trial by fire. I wonder about my future
in the platoon.

That night in the Tigers' Den over a beer, Pete takes a drag on his ciga-
rette, turns towards me and says, "How did you think it went today?"

"My three landings at the end of the day really sucked," I respond.

"You'll get the hang of landing these crates. They're a lot different than
landing a slick. We are dragging them off the runway on takeoff and flying
them right on the edge most of the time. You notice how the EGT is often
right below the red line. That's because the engines are tired, it's hot and
humid here, and we are using all of the power we can get just to get them in
the air. They are heavy to start with, with full fuel, and then we load them
over gross weight with all that ammo and they fly like shit. When you are
dragging them down the runway on takeoff, sometimes the sparks will fly
from the skids scraping the ground, and you will be easing them into translational lift and takeoff. And when you come in with ammo and almost full
fuel, they are one heavy mother to stop. The momentum will carry them all
the way down the runway and off the other end if you don't start slowing
them down as soon as you cross the airfield boundary."

"You know you did the wrong thing on that operation today by not firing the first time at the VC with the AK-47 in black. You could have cost us the lives of the crew or the loss of our ship. You have to decide if you can do this, because we are going to be doing this kind of shit almost every single day."

After a few beers and when it is clear that the most senior commissioned officers have drifted off to their hooches and only the warrants, lieutenants, and a captain remain, a song, like spontaneous combustion, explodes from the remaining warrant officers and lieutenants.

Oh Soc Trang

(To the Tune of "Sweet Betsy from Pike")

Oh Soc Trang Oh Soc Trang's a hell of a place
The organization's a fucking disgrace
With captains and majors and light colonels too
Who sit on the runway with nothing to do.
They scream and they holler they yell and they shout
About many things they know nothing about.
For all of the good they ever will be
They should be shoveling shit on the Isle of Capri.

(As everyone raises their drink for the conclusion)

Aaaaaaaaaaaaaaaaaaaaaamen!

*   *   *

I leave the Tigers' Den and walk back to my hooch past the flight line. The crew chiefs are up on the cabins of our B models checking for damage and checking out the rotor systems. The creaky screen door opens and I walk into a room that has a couple of metal bunks, some stereo equipment from the PX, some shelves made out of wood, a couple of old metal school-type lockers, and two rough-made desks and chairs.

Today is a defining day for me. I put my clothes in a pile. The .45 in the Western holster, with the silver bullets lined up in the black leather belt on the chair, looks like it belongs to a cowboy not a pilot. The square .45 doesn't fit very well in the black leather Western holster or with the cowboy belt bought in downtown Soc Trang with leather slots all around it for .45 caliber bullets. I shove it under my bed and lie down on the sweat-stained sheets for a long restless night of reflection.

On the bunk, I start replaying the tapes in my head from today's mission. How could I screw up two of three landings? The crew chief and door gunner really enjoyed those go-arounds. The sounds outside are a strange mix of generators and occasional outgoing artillery rounds. There are some black bugs on the singular overhead light bulb hanging down in my sparsely decorated room, and I look at the rafters above my head and think of the big rats that are around here. I turn out the solitary light bulb.

My semi-conscious mind replays the combat assaults. There was chatter on the radios that added to the cacophony in the cockpit. There is an acquired art form to setting the right volumes on each of the communication radios and the intercom. The aircraft commander sets the tone, and usually the communications are very low-key and mostly business with the crew, the wingman, the ground troops, the artillery, and the commanding officer, directing the mission from overhead. The wingman is on the same VHF channel and flying a helter-skelter pattern behind us down on the deck. The crew comes in on the intercom to call out what they see happening in the LZ.

Tiger Lead is leading the flight of nine slicks and communicates on VHF and monitors the ground troop commander and the forward observer who are on FM radio frequencies. The fire team leader prior to starting the insertion of the slicks consults a different FM frequency for artillery. And finally, there is Armed Forces Radio (Good Morning Vietnam) out of Vung Tau, playing something like "Light My Fire" or "Born to Be Wild" or some other equally motivational rock and roll inspirational anthem in the background during our mission. I'm wondering how I will ever keep it all straight. I will soon learn to listen for each separate transmission and whom it is coming from on the various radios.

My mind's racing. I killed somebody today. I actually saw the guy in black pajamas with an AK-47, he shot at us, and I killed him. How did I do that? I have got to think about this. I could be doing a lot of this in the Vikings.

I am recalling some of my experiences as a slick driver with the Tigers starting out as a pilot and then becoming an aircraft commander, and the 600 hours of in-country experience I have including multiple combat assaults, ash-and-trash missions, and flying a Vietnamese general around to check on his provinces. I have lived through the Tet Offensive of 1968, and my flying experience includes hauling everything from supplies and ammunition to animals and soldiers, American and ARVN, in and out of little outposts, cities, and occasionally another airfield into some far-flung places in the Mekong Delta. I made aircraft commander in slicks and took a few hits on ash-and-trash missions and combat assaults. As a pilot I even went through one engine failure with minimal structural damage to the skids down over the airport at Bac Lieu.

That was fairly exciting in that we were loaded to the roof with anti-tank weapons. That could have been quite a fireworks display if they had cooked off. But being in guns is going to be a whole different ball game.

Mortar attacks are almost a regular occurrence. The VC are sure interested in killing us every day. Now I am expected to scramble out through the incoming mortars and get airborne. No more getting under a bed or heading for a bunker. Tonight I realize what I am in for, and I spend most of the night thinking about whether this is something I can do. And if so, how in the hell am I going do it?

Saint Edward's Seminary feels like it is a long way away, ancient history. I have trained for a year and always from early on in flight school with the ultimate goal of being a gunship pilot. Now the time is here. I want to do this job because it is important, people's lives are at stake, and I know I can do this, all of it. I want to be the best gunship pilot I can be.

Gunship flying is a whole new phase of this adventure with new rules and procedures. Once you are a gunship driver, you are a specialist. You are no longer doing ash-and-trash flying. You are selected as a member of an elite platoon. You wear a black T-shirt under your jungle fatigues and a black beret. You are scrambling out in the night when the mortars are falling and blowing up the airfield and the base personnel and slick pilots are heading for the bunkers.

Halfway through that night, I wake up. I decide how I am going to make sense of this. I figure I will need to have my own ethics, moral code, and personal code of conduct for being a U.S. Army combat helicopter pilot in B model Huey gunships in Vietnam. Some of my rationale includes knowing that in our company area there are not many secrets. We suspect that the women that clean our hooches, the men who cut our hair, the women who do our laundry, and those who work in the Tigers' Den or in the small PX go home each night to family members who are sympathetic to if not directly associated with the Viet Cong. Many civilian Vietnamese workers from the nearby town of Soc Trang, both men and women, work on the airfield, and each day they walk in through gates past the security screening of the military police, and at the end of the day they walk out and back down the road to town and to their homes about a half-mile away.

(In the spring of 1968 it came out that in fact some personnel who worked on our base were caught with crudely drawn maps of the base indicating where the various facilities were located and where the officers and enlisted men lived.)

The housekeepers and laundry workers had access to our personal effects every day. Some Vietnamese worked in the PX or the Tigers' Den, our airfield's officers' club. Some of them walked right by the flight line where our missions were posted and updated. We joked in the bar that the Viet Cong seemed to know where our missions were going before we got there. We didn't know if this was in fact true. But the more I reflected on it, the more likely it seemed that it was. I began listing in my head some basic assumptions for developing my own personal code of conduct. The enemy probably knows what our game plan is. I logically conclude that it is very possible they know exactly where we were going on our missions. The VC are trying each day to shoot down our aircraft and kill us. They regularly engage our slicks and helicopter gunships with rifles, automatic weapons, rockets, and mortars. The rumors abound that there is a bounty on helicopter pilots. Stories circulate of mutilated bodies, of VC and NVA given extra pay or some other form of recognition for having killed one of us.

I develop a specific personal plan. If I come into an operational area with the mission of prepping it for the slicks and I see a VC in black pajamas with a weapon, he will be history. If I am fired upon, I will return fire. If I get an order or request to fire because soldiers are in contact, I will fire whatever is necessary or what I am ordered to fire to cover the soldiers in their operation to allow them to make successful contact or for them to get the hell out of there. If part of the plan for an insertion or pick-up of troops is to "shoot 'em up" because we know from experience that this is a place where the enemy is ready for us, then we will dump the whole nine yards on them and aggressively prep the landing zone. We will do whatever needs to be done to make the place as safe as possible for the slicks and the ground troops.

* * *

I am trying to remember what I learned, if anything, in the seminary about war. What the hell! I'm a pilot and soldier in the middle of this war. As far as I know the potential spread of communism is real, and, besides, it's not my place to determine this. That's for someone in a higher pay grade than me to figure out. I am a helicopter gunship pilot and I will do the best job I can in this role.

We are definitely involved in a war. We believe strongly that what we are doing is right. I believe if I buy the farm, at least I am doing something worthwhile and necessary. I decide I can do this! This is the job I signed on to do, and now I am actually doing it. This is the adventure I was looking for. Maybe it's a little more than I was expecting, but there's no turning back now. This is the most difficult thing I have ever done in my life. I can do this. I will do this. My fellow flight crewmembers and the troops we are supporting down in the rice paddies and out in the jungles are counting on me.

I will take on this responsibility and do the best I can to carry out my orders and do this difficult work every day I am here. Once I thought this through and made my decision I approached my new responsibilities with a deep sense of commitment and responsibility. My goal not only became to become a skilled helicopter gunship pilot but to one day become a fire team leader in our platoon.

Soc Trang, Vietnam
Thursday, May 23, 1968

Dear Mom, Dad, and Family,

    … I'm now in the gun platoon. I fly left seat and have a gun sight that controls 4 M-60 machine guns on flexible pylon mounts. The man flying right seat fires the rockets and does all the flying and communicating when we go down to tree top level. Then I fire the machine guns and am there if he should get hit … a whole new type of flying and the aircraft commander has much responsibility coordinating with transports on combat assaults and with the ground troops when they get in hot water and need some close fire support. It seemed like I knew the game as an aircraft commander in slicks but now I'm on the ground floor again as one of the new pilots in guns. You have to sacrifice a little to learn a little different aspect of this game. Now I will train to become an aircraft commander of a wing ship in a two-ship fire team and eventually maybe become a fire team leader if it turns out that I can catch on fast enough and have enough time left in country at that point. There are a few more tight situations to deal with and this offers a much greater challenge I think than slicks did.… So long for now. Will write again soon.

Love,
Your Son, Fred

2

A Family Tradition

This book is a story about the Vietnam War. It is also a personal story. I was there for one year from December 17, 1967, to December 17, 1968. I was 21 years old when I arrived and turned 22 during my ninth month in-country. I flew 1,300 hours of missions as a U.S. Army warrant officer and helicopter pilot. They say timing is everything. I had been in-country for about a month and a half when, on Tuesday, January 30, 1968, the Tet Offensive started. During the next couple of months, we literally lived in our helicopters, flying missions whenever we were needed, and sleeping under them at night.

The purpose of the Tet Offensive from the point of view of the enemy, the Viet Cong (VC) and North Vietnamese Army regulars (NVA), was to strike military and civilian command centers in South Vietnam, incite the population to overturn the Vietnamese government, and end the war in a single offensive blow. They had done something similar successfully before in their war with the French over colonial oppression at Dien Bien Phu in 1954. Now we were on the receiving end of very aggressive fighting and vigorous coordinated operations by the Viet Cong and North Vietnamese Army regulars to attack airfields, support installations, cities, towns, and personnel throughout Vietnam in a unified and highly orchestrated offensive. They were out to win the war on our watch.

In this book I will sometimes use names or alternate names of my fellow pilots and crewmembers for a number of reasons. I didn't want to leave anybody out. I didn't want to say uncomfortable things about people. The experiences in this book were mine, and others might not have seen them or felt them this way. I have changed a few names or used only a first name or nickname in some of the writing to protect privacy. Every one of us made mistakes, miscalculations, or questionable decisions at some point in our tour. Each person makes their own sense of a war, and it is not my place to project or imply that my thoughts or actions were any better or worse than anyone else's. I know I made a number of mistakes in combat. Some were funny and some were downright stupid, dangerous, and scary. I knew a little about myself when I was 21, and I had a lot more to learn about life, war, and myself. I enlisted to be a helicopter pilot expecting to go to Vietnam. With that enlistment came these experiences.

I was stationed at Soc Trang Army Airfield adjacent to the city of Soc Trang. The city was formerly named Khang Hung during the Japanese occupation of Vietnam. Our airfield was located in the IV Corps (southern sector) area of the country. We supported ARVN companies and the Ninth Infantry Division. Sometimes we also worked with Special Forces units and infantry advisors in various outposts. We also supported what was called the "Brown Water Navy" whose boats patrolled the rivers and streams of the Mekong Delta. Their own gunships, the Seawolves, were sometimes down for maintenance or they needed relief. The enemy forces we encountered were predominantly Viet Cong. Occasionally, like during the Tet Offensive of 1968, or along the Seven Mountains area by the Cambodian border, we encountered North Vietnamese Army regulars (NVA) who had come down the Ho Chi Minh Trail from North Vietnam to support the local Viet Cong.

The stories, poems, and writings in this book are true to the best of my recollection and ability. I've done my best to recall them in as much detail as possible. I have resisted the temptation to make them more than they were. We had plenty of daily adventures and experiences so there wasn't a need to write fiction for a compelling story.

I have to say it was the most exciting adventure of my life. The job I had in Vietnam involved some things that are difficult to talk about. Many war veterans prefer not to talk about their combat experiences at all. I respect their decisions. It is sometimes difficult to share stories with people who have not been in combat. It has been my experience that people will say that they want to hear your story. But then you have to hold short of all of the details because they don't want to hear that much. I wanted to tell my story and how I processed it so my family could understand why I have a few quirky behaviors and with the hope that others might understand what being in combat was like for me.

I came with excellent training and mental preparedness from the U.S. Army, but nothing in that training prepared me for the moral dilemmas and life-and-death decisions that needed to be made to survive and thrive on a daily basis as a helicopter pilot in the Vietnam War. I was grateful to my parents, who were both U.S. Army officers, and for the discipline and comprehensive education that I received starting at Saint Patrick's Elementary School, in Tacoma, Washington, and through the first semester of my first year of college at Saint Edward's Seminary in Kenmore, Washington, northeast of Seattle.

During this adventure I made the transition from being a Catholic school student, altar boy, seminarian, and relatively timid, reserved, and inexperienced young person to becoming a seasoned, disciplined, and proficient combat helicopter pilot. I was a naive and relatively sheltered young man when I entered the Army. I was a very average student in school and in fact found most of school to be very boring. When I received the silver wings of an Army aviator, I naively thought to myself, "I am going to savor this moment, because it is the last time I may ever graduate from a school of any kind."

*   *   *

I bought a ring with my class number 67–19, the 19th class of helicopter pilots to graduate in 1967, that I wear to this day. Little did I know that later in life I would attend four colleges and universities, obtain a doctorate, and spend a career as a schoolteacher and a school administrator, school superintendent, college instructor, author, and the mayor of a city.

If I had been a more diligent student of history during high school, maybe I would have understood more about the country of Vietnam, its people, and in particular the history of its people enduring wars and much suffering over hundreds of years of colonial oppression under the rule of the French and Japanese. But then again, not much of this information was included in our old history books because the escalation of the war started quietly and was so new.

I did bring some core values and a very basic sense of philosophy, theology, ethics, and moral decision-making to my role as an Army warrant officer from my immersion in the classical education I received at Seattle Prep and Saint Edward's Seminary. This background was important to me for processing the experiences and for coming out of them at peace with the decisions I made, the actions I took, and the part I played in the war.

In addition to flying responsibilities, I was our base's assistant civic actions officer, charged to be a liaison with a hospital, orphanage, and Chieu Hoi center (POW retraining camp) in the town of Soc Trang. I was also the editor of the company newsletter called *The Tiger's Tail*, assistant public information officer, and the awards and decorations officer. I would write up recommendations for our commanding officer to approve and submit for the achievements of our pilots and helicopter crewmen on various missions.

In the Army, people have multiple assignments, and senior officers assign you what they think you can handle and what you are good at. There is much more to do to keep an assault helicopter company operational than just flying missions. Many of us did whatever was needed to get the job done.

I felt very fortunate to be assigned to the 121st Assault Helicopter

Company. Our company was a high-performance company with quality leadership and dedicated pilots and support crewmembers. We were proud of our history and traditions and the fact that others could count on us to get the job done and do the difficult missions that we were regularly called on to accomplish. We had great reputation to uphold and did our best to do this on every assigned mission.

As strange as some people may find it, for the most part I really enjoyed my time in the Army and at Soc Trang. It was an experience that was transformational and defining for me in terms of becoming an adult. My self-image was transformed, and my capacity for leadership in the future grew significantly.

I have a deep, abiding respect and compassion for veterans and especially for anyone who served in Vietnam. Now that extends to those soldiers who have served and are serving in the more recent wars in Iraq and Afghanistan. I feel we owe a great debt of gratitude to the soldiers who did this, honoring the commitments they made and believing their efforts were helping to preserve life, liberty, and the pursuit of happiness for the citizens of this great country of ours.

As veterans, many of us care deeply about the people whose lives were destroyed in the process of fighting this war. Those veterans who lived and returned to civilian life suffering from their wartime experiences, defining events, or series of experiences deserve full access to their VA benefits and the health care and mental health counseling.

My thoughts at the time of my own service were that, when it comes to pulling the trigger, we need to have the most sensitive and rational people making those kinds of life-and-death decisions. I considered myself to be that kind of person. The last thing an assault helicopter company needs is a trigger-happy whack job on the end of a mini gun that shoots hundreds of rounds in a few seconds. This may sound sort of crazy in a civilian context. One of the first lessons you learn in war is that some things about war don't make any sense, especially to the combat soldier.

As I completed my one-year tour of duty in Vietnam I didn't believe we were winning the Vietnam War. In many cases it seemed like we won various battles only to go back into the same areas multiple times and repeat the same process with similar results.

Early in my education career after Vietnam, through some very valuable staff development training called "Human Effectiveness Training," I learned some essential skills for "controlling the self-talk" in my head and looking for "opportunity in every difficulty." I hope we came away as a country more enlightened about the complexity and atrocity of war and the importance of not assuming that our ways and beliefs will necessarily work or should be imposed on other cultures and peoples.

I haven't really seen our country's current actions reflect that under-standing ... yet. I am optimistic that one day they will. Politicians will make significantly different decisions about military action if they have been per-sonally involved as soldiers in war. Too many of our current politicians are eager to commit others to going to war but have never been in the military themselves to know the implications of what they are recommending.

*   *   *

The men and women I flew with and supported were very courageous and dedicated soldiers. Some of them made the ultimate sacrifice by lay-ing down their lives in this war. No one can ever take away those acts of courage that are etched into our minds or the sacrifices that we saw them make on a regular basis. They were dedicated, hardworking, and willing to risk their lives for the mission and for their friends. A number of helicop-ter pilots who were with us in Soc Trang, and those who were my friends and flight school classmates who served in other units, gave their lives in this war.

I don't know why I have been given the privilege of these additional 50 plus years of living. I am 74 as I finish writing this book. I have had a very memorable career of public service in education and municipal govern-ment and a very full and rewarding life after Vietnam. This book will reveal some things about me that others may not have known while I was active in my positions in education, municipal government or my church. I ask peo-ple to reflect and realize that war is a very unique and different reality expe-rience from normal life.

The framework for this book came from the letters and poems I wrote home regularly to family members and that my mother saved. My mother and father were the real deal. National newscaster Tom Brokaw accurately described my parents' generation in his book *The Greatest Generation*. They were very proud of their military service and the part they played in con-fronting and defeating the aggression of both Japan's and Germany's leaders in World War II. I felt like in a small way I was continuing the family tradi-tion of serving in the U.S. Army as an officer and giving part of my life for a noble cause.

Mom was an Army nurse, and my dad was a lieutenant colonel in supply and logistics in the Army. They met in the jungles of New Guinea. She was also an artist, a dancer, a writer, an entertainer, and the very best mother ever to me. She approached life with enthusiasm, creativity, and humor. She also had dyslexia and struggled to overcome it and its impli-cations for how she felt about herself, her life, and her writing. She taught me to enjoy life, laugh loudly and often, love writing, do arts and crafts projects, and dabble in the art of painting pictures with words. She had a mother's sixth sense that the letters I wrote home would be of significant value to me someday, and so she saved them. I can't tell her how much that gesture means to me now because she died on May 20, 2007, at the age of 90. My father died the previous year, on May 4, 2006, at the age of 92. They both died with family members present and were courageous, tough, and filled with faith, optimism, humor, and hope until the very end.

There was a sense of awe and amazement in the eyes of my brother and sisters, spouse and grandchildren, when each of my parents was given a separate burial with full military honors at Tahoma National Cemetery in the shadow of Mount Rainier in western Washington. When the disciplined, polished, and respectful honor guard folded the American flag and presented it to one of my siblings, and the soldiers collected the spent rifle shells from the 21-gun salutes and gave them to family members, it was an experience we will never forget. The funeral director, who was an old seminary buddy of mine, had tears in his eyes on these occasions. Our family has done its part in the U.S. military and to a great degree, our lives and personal character traits were formed by many of our Army experiences in a combat theater.

I have been deeply privileged to have had my parents, brother and sisters, and extended family support me throughout my life and in particular when I was in Vietnam. Someday, my remains and my wife Shannon's remains will be placed where my parents are interred at Tahoma National Cemetery in the State of Washington with a spectacular view of Mount Rainier, and the circle of my own life will be completed.

*   *   *

My brother, John McCarthy, is a risk-taker and survivor in his own right and someone I admire for his sense of adventure and positive attitude. As a youngster he overcame hearing issues, which he accommodated and took in stride for his whole life.

He started out in the shipping department of a major pharmaceutical company and worked there for 50 years, rising to the position of distribution centers auditor. His email signature includes the following quote attributed to Helen Keller: "Life is either a daring adventure or nothing at all." I have had a few daring adventures along the way as well. Vietnam was certainly at the top of my list.

I was born on September 24, 1946, in Tacoma, Washington. When I look at Mom's picture, through the eyes of a child, I can see how attractive she was and how much she loved me. I was my parents' first child, and after me would come three sisters and one brother. Mom had a laugh that would light up a party and shake the rafters. Occasionally it was a little embarrassing for me. She loved a well-made Manhattan, telling jokes, laughing, singing, and dancing. She was quite a seamstress and creative person and liked to paint pictures with words as well as with paintbrushes. She braided our dining room carpet out of colorful rags she had collected. While in the service, she had some of her poems about military life published in *Army Times*. Later in life, her humor and writing talent manifested itself in a funny memoir she wrote, titled *Jungle Rot and Khaki Bloomers*. I'm sure she had lots of admirers in the Army.

As an Army nurse during World War II, she was surrounded by men. Many of them were infatuated with her because she tended to them, was frequently laughing, and, as she said later in life, had learned how to do nursing the high-touch way: she gave backrubs and hugged people and could make a bed with hospital corners. She grew up in an Army family in Wyckoff, New Jersey. Her father, a no-nonsense army captain who worked at the Port of Hoboken, New Jersey, sent supplies and men off in troop ships. Her mother tended to her housework, loved gardening, and read the Bible regularly. A few days after Mom graduated from high school her father took her to a school in Elizabeth, New Jersey, and said, "Betty, you are going to be a nurse." She didn't argue with him. Her childhood had been one of obedience to her father, but also one of playing in the local woods, swimming in the creek, catching fireflies at night in jars, helping her mother with housework, and looking up to her adventurous and quirky older sister, Charlotte. Charlotte wrote poetry, as did my mother. Writing was a joy for them growing up in rural New Jersey. Occasionally she did babysit for a boy who lived next door and later became the world-famous and well-known bandleader Nelson Riddle.

We once visited my mom's family home when I was about 10 years old. I remember the flight in a four-engine DC 6. I also remember my uncle having me get into the bucket of his backhoe while he drove it around the driveway at his home. The screen door on Gramma Itzen's country cottage slammed open and closed as we went in and out to play in the yard. I remember that we sat on the rail fence in her backyard, catching fireflies in jars and watching a thunderstorm that scared the daylights out of us. I can still see the well-worn wood floors of their weathered home, smell the flowers, and feel the experience of visiting the home where my mother grew up.

Our family on my father's side had come out from North Dakota to settle in Tacoma, Washington. Life in the Dakotas had not been easy. An uncle had homesteaded in a sod house on the prairie. My father was a serious and intent person, who worked hard and enjoyed his family. He was an active Catholic. He loved to have friends over, have a drink, and sing Irish songs. His own dad died when he was 12 years old, so he had to grow up early. He and his sister, Bernadette, helped their mother run a couple of movie theaters in Fargo and Mandan, North Dakota. My dad took the tickets, and his sister played the piano to accompany the scenes during the silent movies. When the family moved out West to Tacoma, they all decided to live in proximity to each other.

Dad graduated from North Dakota State University in electrical engineering and Army ROTC. When he met my mother in the jungles of New Guinea during World War II, he had received a war promotion and was a lieutenant colonel in charge of a supply company. He looked sort of like General Eisenhower, from a caricature one of his men drew, and had an understated toughness about him. For a number of years, I thought he was way too serious most of the time and he wasn't much fun. I now realize occasionally I must seem a lot like him.

Our Great Uncle Jim had been the stationmaster of the impressive Union Pacific train station in Tacoma, Washington. In the early 1950s, train stations were grand architectural structures and considered the gateway to a thriving city. Tacoma's was no exception. The family story was that Great Uncle Jim had lost a leg under a train as a conductor earlier in life. One of my other uncles, Pat Howe, was a train engineer. My grandmother worked in the shipyards during World War II and then lived most of her life with my Uncle Jerry and his wife, and her daughter, Bernadette, and their family of three boys. She made the best orange rolls we would enjoy on our Sunday visits. I had aunts, uncles, and cousins from five very close families that lived within about six blocks of each other. My uncle Fred's son, Fritz, was a good friend of my dad. They would hunt jackrabbits together with a 1916 Winchester 22 that my father gave to me. Fritz was a graduate of West Point. He was an infantry lieutenant and was captured by the Japanese during World War II. He was on a Japanese POW ship that was bombed by the Americans and was killed in the attack. I know it must have been a very difficult experience for my dad to lose his childhood friend and relative this way. My father was the recipient of the Legion of Merit award for his wartime service and leadership ability.

I have great memories of growing up in that Tacoma neighborhood as a young child. There were many backyard picnics with my cousins, listening to the older folks talk about some of the hardships they had left in the Dakotas and their interest in each other's families. My Uncle Jerry was a great jokester and enjoyed pulling pranks on everyone. I remember a time when he and Uncle Fred were comparing salmon just caught in Tacoma's Commencement Bay for size and weight. As Uncle Jerry's tipped the scale, he got a funny look on his face and then burst out laughing. He had filled the salmon with lead weights from his tackle box when Uncle Fred wasn't looking. He was a talented woodworker, and one Christmas I was given a gas station model that he had created out of plywood and painted with the Texaco signs. It was a prized possession during my childhood. Whenever we needed something in those days we looked first to family for help. When teeth were loose, Uncle Jerry had a special pair of chrome pliers, and he would pull out our loose teeth.

Everyone in each of the families supported each other, and four of the five families went to Saint Patrick's Catholic Church on Sunday. Our families got together at least once a month at somebody's house for meals and fun. It was a great way to grow up, feeling so connected and supported in our extended family.

*   *   *

We moved from Tacoma to Seattle, Washington, in 1953 when I was seven years old. My father was a partner in the Bearing Sales and Service Company, and they were expanding and needed his skills in the Seattle area. My parents bought a grand old brick home in the Magnolia Bluff neighborhood northwest of the downtown area of Seattle.

The house was a two-story red brick home with an unfinished basement. It sat on a raised corner lot on an arterial with a bus stop across the street and a separate two-car brick garage for our one car.

Mom never got a driver's license and preferred to ride the bus into downtown Seattle for her shopping trips. Magnolia is a self-contained neighborhood separated from the city of Seattle by two concrete bridges. We attended the local Catholic elementary school four blocks away, played with other kids in the neighborhood, and wandered all over Magnolia exploring the many interesting parts of our neighborhood within the city but miles away because of its geographical separation from the downtown area of Seattle. Magnolia was a village of a few businesses, churches, parks, tennis courts, and beautiful views of the water. Fort Lawton, an Army fort, was located on the northwest side of Magnolia. We enjoyed exploring there but were always under the watchful eyes of the Army military police. There were housing areas, firing ranges, parade grounds, and a movie theater we could go to with an Army connected friend for 25 cents. We brought our own popcorn in paper sacks. We went fishing for sole and flounder with sandworms off West Point by the fort when the tide was low, and Mom would cook the fish when we got home.

There wasn't much traffic in Magnolia because it was a residential neighborhood separated from the city of Seattle. People didn't come there generally unless they lived there, were visiting friends, or were just enjoying a Sunday drive along Magnolia Boulevard. The boulevard was where many of the architectural jewels of Magnolia were located. Each home had impressively manicured grounds and spectacular sweeping views of the city, Puget Sound, ferries, sailboats, container ships, the downtown skyline, and the world-famous Seattle Space Needle. We lived across a small valley to the east, on the top of what was called by our parents "mortgage hill." We had a nice view of Puget Sound from the upstairs bedroom windows. My brother and I had a room, and my sisters had their own room as well. Life was generally very good for me.

After elementary school, I went to my first year of high school at Seattle Prep, at that time an all-boys Jesuit high school, across town. As a freshman, I played basketball on the second-string team, called the Cubs. My year of riding the bus across town for high school was an early regular adventure out of my familiar neighborhood. It included transferring buses in the downtown area of Seattle and riding to the school located on Capitol Hill. I got a new coat for school, made of green fake leather. I was the smallest kid in my entering freshman class.

At Seattle Prep, during my freshman year of high school, the Jesuits taught us, among other valuable teachings and disciplines, religion. I remember a life-long guiding principle that I learned early on from the Jesuits for making sense of the precepts of Catholic Church teaching and for processing life's adventures, challenges, and important decisions: "An informed conscience is the highest form of moral judgment." This guidepost, for a reflective teenaged individual, provided a logical rationale for accepting the contradictions that existed in my mind about war. It also placed an expectation on me to study and learn and inform my own conscience. It left the ultimate decision-making up to me. This theology seemed to make sense to me even at the early age of 15. As I have grown into an adult, my view of life allows me to be an active participant, who thrives on involvement, leadership opportunities, and regular spiritual experiences, while taking exception with a number of formal positions in my Church that don't pass the informed conscience test for me.

Somewhere along the line I decided that I wanted to become a priest. After my freshman year at Seattle Prep, I transferred to Saint Edward's Seminary, a boarding school about 20 miles away from Magnolia on 360 tree-covered acres on the north shore of Lake Washington. During my time in school there, I received a comprehensive classical liberal arts education and additional classes in Gregorian chant, Latin, Greek, and French, as well as philosophy, religion, theology, science and mathematics. Students also participated in a rigorous intramural physical education program in the major sports of football, basketball, baseball, and track. Study, silence, discipline, reflection, and prayer characterized student life. These educational and life experiences were important to me personally back then and in the later unfolding destiny of my life and the adventures that were in my future. I was fortunate to have had many good teachers and mentors among my classmates and the upperclassmen in our school.

Sometimes people ask me what possessed me to go to the seminary. I have to say that we were raised Catholics and I got to know many sisters and priests who seemed to enjoy teaching and helping people, and they had a sense of purpose and dedication in their work. Some were family friends like Tacoma Dominican Sister Mary James, an educator whom my mother and father always treated with the utmost respect. She was such a joy-filled person, and perhaps it was the peace I saw in her eyes and in the priests I knew that tipped the scales for me. Or maybe it was my first cousin, Father Tom Bunnell, a life-long Jesuit, who was such an important part of our extended family and whom my parents always held in high regard. My parents never said they wanted me to follow this path, but they were supportive of my choices financially and personally and always encouraged me to do my best at whatever I did.

* * *

When I joined the Army, I realized fairly early on that I had had a rather different high school experience compared to most of my fellow trainees and warrant officer candidates. I believe the education and training I received in excellent Catholic schools prepared me uniquely for Army life, and also gave me some basic tools for making the difficult moral and ethical judgments that are necessary for life in the military. The seminary was a boarding school, so I was comfortable living with other men and being on my own. The golden rule values I learned in parochial school are applicable anywhere, and I had already learned how to get along with quite a few different people.

I believed the war was justified when I entered the United States Army and was involved in it. I came from a family with a long history of decorated combat service in the U.S. Army. My mother, father, an uncle, and a grandfather were all U.S. Army officers. I didn't really have a clear sense about what the combat experience would be like when I enlisted in the Army in December of 1966. I don't think anyone does. I only knew I loved flying, I wanted some adventure in my life, and I thought I would be risking my life for a noble cause.

I arrived in-country in Vietnam at 21 years of age, one month before all hell broke loose during the Tet Offensive of January 1968. I flew 1,300 hours of flight missions during my one-year tour. I served with a unit that had a history of quality combat performance and a record of courageous, dedicated service. Serving as a Tiger with Soc Trang Tigers as a pilot and then aircraft commander and in the Viking Platoon as a Viking, first as pilot, and then as an aircraft commander and fire team leader, was a special privilege. Hanoi Hannah called our gunship platoon the "Blue Diamond Devils of the Delta" for the wrath that our gunships could rain down on the enemy. As a fire team leader, my call sign was "Viking 23."

In the Vikings we had a very well developed standard operating procedure that we were taught and that we taught others. This was an essential piece in our being able to respond and to fly our missions in difficult circumstances, with a high degree of mission success and risk management.

Jerry Daly, a chief warrant officer who was just finishing one of his tours as I arrived in the unit, emphasized this SOP. He had been an Army aviator since 1959. His flight experience included 4,900 total hours of flight time; 2,100 hours were in helicopter gunships. On March 26, 1967, he was involved in a joint airmobile assault with multiple assets from two helicopter companies and the battalion commander. Four helicopters were shot down in the landing zone. Among those killed was the battalion commander, Col. Dempsey. Eleven gunships were scrambled from the assault helicopter companies in the Delta. Chief Warrant Officer Daly commanded a Viking helicopter modified to lay down a smoke screen so the survivors could be rescued. He joined up with the gunships and made 13 runs laying down smoke amidst heavy enemy fire. The survivors were rescued by a Dustoff medevac helicopter and three slicks. The helicopter took so many hits that when the mission was accomplished, it was determined to be unflyable and was red Xed from further flight. The losses that day were 142 enemy dead, 42 ARVN dead, 69 ARVN wounded, 12 American wounded, four Americans dead, and four helicopters destroyed.

He went on to serve multiple tours and was one of the most decorated U.S. Army helicopter pilots in the Vietnam War. He was a detail person, disciplined, and known for his courage and knowledge of the inner workings of the Huey and its armament systems as well as his intuitive sense of the aircraft's capabilities. After the war he became a Catholic priest. Our lives were in good hands because of his diligence in implementing our standard operating procedures.

*   *   *

A seminary is a school for training young men to be Catholic priests. I entered Saint Edward's Seminary in Kenmore, Washington, on the north end of Lake Washington, northeast of Seattle, in 1961, in my sophomore year of high school. I spent most of my elementary school years in Catholic school. I spent my freshman year of high school at Seattle Prep on Capitol Hill in Seattle, where I benefited from the academic rigor of the Jesuits. Among a long list of core values they instilled in me were discipline, hard work, preparing for my lessons, and a good vocabulary from memorizing 10 vocabulary words a week. As I mentioned earlier, they also taught me to question authority. Not theirs, however. Discipline was ever-present in the form of a priest disciplinarian who carried around a piece of rubber hose off a dishwasher and didn't hesitate to use it if the student offense warranted a good whack.

Catholic school experience is a part of me. I knew priests, sisters, and brothers whom I admired, and at a very young age I wanted to give my own life in service to others. I wanted to experience the joy I saw in their faces, and to live with the simplicity and integrity I saw in their daily lives. Later in life these simple beliefs would be tested in a number of ways, but they formed the basis for a later adult set of Catholic beliefs.

In the seminary we lived in a classic old Gothic building. It was made of brick, stone, and concrete, and conjured up thoughts of celestial grandeur and clerical significance. We lived there for nine months of the year, going home only occasionally for a weekend pass and at Christmas, Easter, and in the summer. There were six grades at Saint Edward's. There were four grades of high school and two grades of college. Each class had about 25 to 30 students in it. There were about 150 students at Saint Ed's. It was called the minor seminary. We had some good teachers and some great teachers, and they expected and got a lot out of us. Father Farrell, Father Healy, and Father McManus were all iconic figures in our lives. I always thought they were looking at me with a bit of a skeptical eye and thinking, "What's this McCarthy guy doing here anyway?"

My academic performance was average at best because my mind was often on some sports contest, hiking, playing the guitar, or other adventure when I was not in class. I was a good writer and got good grades for my written work. In the subject areas of mathematics and science, I was a little challenged. I had a lot of friends and generally it was a positive experience for me. Life on the outside was considered by our professors to be too secular, so the possession of a transistor radio could result in dismissal. We lived above the first floor where the classrooms and refectory (dining hall) were located. The "rule of silence" prevailed above the first floor, and we were expected to not talk above the first floor, where we lived in small dorm-type rooms with a roommate. We were supposed to use a simplified form of hand signals to indicate what we were asking for in our rooms or at meals eaten mostly in silence.

About a quarter of a mile away, on the same grounds, was another building, more modern than Saint Edward's, that housed the major seminary. Its name was Saint Thomas Seminary, and it had students for six grades also, two years of college and four years of theology. The two seminaries together involved 12 years of education and culminated with ordination as a priest. The two schools sat on 360 acres of pristine northwest timbered lands and trails on the north end of Lake Washington. It was a dream come true for a boy who loved hiking and the outdoors and the freedom of being on his own, away from the perceived limits of home life in the city of Seattle.

We went to school six days a week in the seminary. Saturday was just like Monday through Friday. We were in regular classes on Saturday. Each day we had two hours to recreate from 3:00 to 5:00 p.m. We always looked forward to and made the most of that two-hour time frame. Each evening we had a supervised silent study hall from 7:00 to 8:30 p.m. The rule of silence prevailed during study hall also. A priest would monitor the study hall and walk up and down the aisles between the desks. We could raise our hands and whisper questions or ask for permission to walk down the hallway to the bathroom. Sometimes the supervising priest would surprise a student who had dozed off at his desk with a whack of a ruler on the desk. It was for me a place to study, do my homework, and learn who I was and what I was about.

Everyone was required to play every sport in our school. We had the ultimate intramural program that was thought out in minute detail by the priests who organized our school. There were five teams with eight strings on each team. The names of the teams were the Buccaneers, the Crusaders, the Centurions, the Spartans, and the Vikings. I was a Viking, and that proved to be a prophetic team name for me in my military future.

A second-year college man led each team. He was the team captain, and a first-year college man was the assistant team captain. We played the sports of football, basketball, baseball, track and field, and cross-country. Every student was expected to participate in every sport. The design of the intramural program was highly motivational. An eighth-string game was worth a few less points than a first-string game. The first-string players were the equivalent of high school varsity players, and the eighth-string players were less skilled in sports. The first-string players went to the other string level games to cheer them on. I was a first-string player and a fairly good athlete. The points for each game and each season were carefully counted and regularly reported. At the end of the school year the coveted status of school champions was awarded to the team with the most accumulated points. We played our hearts out in those games, and everyone's participation was valued and appreciated. First-string players mentored eighth-string players to get more points for their team. It was an excellent peer-mentoring model for students.

Life in the seminary included spiritual exercises, mortification (a term I never did fully understand but it sounded pretty profound) and self-denial. We went to mass every day and two times on Sunday. The main school building had four floors, an imposing bell tower, and a basement area with locker rooms, a baggage storage area, and science classrooms. The rest of the classrooms were on the first floor. The halls on the first floor were lined with the ordination pictures of past graduating classes of priests going back in history for the Archdiocese of Seattle to the early years of the 20th century.

We lived on the second, third and fourth floors of the school in small college dorm-type rooms with a sink, two desks, two bunks, built-in storage, and a roommate. We were bound by the "rule of silence" like many monasteries and seminaries, and we were instructed not to speak above the first floor. The rules were designed to keep the world at bay.

We ate some of our meals in silence in a large formal dining area called a "refectory" on the first floor. Everything at the seminary had a lofty designation consistent with high expectations for students. Sometimes we were allowed to talk, but most of the time a student was selected to read books about the martyrs and saints or some other piece of selected (and screened by our professors) quality contemporary literature. One of the more interesting approved books was *Profiles in Courage* by John F. Kennedy. I remember an incident when one of our classmates, Larry, was a reader. As he read from the martyrology (stories of Church martyrs) from the podium that looked like the rostrum in a cathedral, we heard the names of some of our fellow students interspersed with the saints' stories in funny ways that the professors didn't pick up on but the students enjoyed immensely.

The faculty professors sat on a raised platform above the students and were waited on by older students. It was quite an honor to be a waiter. After serving, you got to eat the same food as the professors. We might be served hamburger or chicken fried steak while they were served sirloin steaks. As students we learned to be polite, work hard, and play hard to earn the respect of our fellow students. I learned my place in the hierarchy of Saint Edward's Seminary. We all knew that we could leave at any time, but generally we enjoyed life at the school and most of my classmates stayed during the years I was there. Sometimes a student would leave in the middle of the night and we were not told why. In retrospect, it could have been for a rule violation, for having what was called a "particular friendship" with another student that was considered unhealthy, or because they just decided that they no longer wanted to be there.

There were no choices of classes in the seminary. We all took a healthy dose of classical education. We took Religion, Latin, Greek, French and Gregorian Chant, in addition to regular high school courses of Chemistry, Physics, Science, Mathematics, English, and Social Studies. By the time I finished high school, I was tired of the isolated academic rigor and was ready for some sort of adventure out in the "real world," as we called life on the outside of the seminary walls. Occasionally we were allowed a half day off to hike in the woods or to walk to the town of Kenmore about two miles away with an older student chaperone. One of the great adventures there included a go-cart racetrack.

I enjoyed the silence and contemplative atmosphere of the seminary, but I was really ready for some of the adventures I had read about in books. I was becoming interested in cars and motorcycles and longed to drive and own them. Also, I was getting interested in what it would be like to be going out with girls. A student named Jack transferred into the seminary from a Catholic high school in Seattle during his senior year, and he was a very engaging character. He had an immaculate, jet-black 1957 Chevy hardtop that he managed to hide in the woods on the seminary property, and he had lots of friends in and around Seattle. He was very popular with the girls who attended an all-girls Catholic high school, many of whom were cheerleaders for his former all-boys school. When we got the opportunity for some time off, he introduced us to his friends from the city, and among them were a number of girls. This was an exciting time for us and opened all sorts of new doors and experiences for many of us.

I left the seminary halfway through my first year of college, in January of 1965. It was the time of the semester break, and I just didn't see going any further down this path at this time in my life. I went to work part-time for my father, who had an electrical contracting and appliance repair business in downtown Seattle. I decided that it was time to pursue some of my goals and to explore other areas of interest. My first vehicle while I was still in the seminary was a red Cushman Super Eagle motor scooter with a large dice for a shifter. Later I would buy a number of cars I had admired, including a maroon 1957 Chevrolet convertible and a 1955 Ford hardtop in classic turquoise and white. I enrolled in Shoreline Community College because my mom knew someone who worked there. He was the head of the police academy training program. I had a great deal of respect for police officers and the difficult work they did each day but I really wasn't interested in becoming one.

I also applied for and was hired to work at Evergreen Washelli Cemetery. During this time of starting community college on "the outside," I had a teacher who encouraged my writing ability. As a result of his mentorship, I had some poems published in the school literary magazine and even had a couple of them read by a local radio icon on KIXI Seattle's Sunday night FM radio show "Reflections." The program started with the music "Clair de Lune," and then the poetry was read. Some of those poems are included in this book.

The Vietnam War was in the news. I told my friends I thought a lot about learning to fly. One of them said, "You always talk about doing adventurous things, but you don't ever seem to do them." That was all of the challenge that I needed. I found out that flying lessons were offered in

Everett, Washington, and I signed up for ground school and started taking flight lessons in a Cessna 150. I enjoyed the feeling of flying an airplane and controlling it in three dimensions. Mathematics seemed to come alive for the first time for me when applied to aerodynamics and flight planning. I soloed a Cessna 150 in 1966 at Paine Field at a flight school called Cal Aero. My instructor was an interesting fellow named Bill, who was a member of the widely known Northwest Weyerhaeuser Lumber Company family, and I believe he ultimately became a bush pilot in Alaska. Soloing was an extraordinary experience for me. It started me thinking about being a pilot and maybe even someday flying in the military.

One day I took the bus into downtown Seattle. I had ridden that bus many times down Second Avenue to the Garment District where I had taken a job in a jacket factory. Today was different. I had seen an Army recruiter's storefront on a street named Pike between Second and First avenue, and the pictures in the windows got me thinking that maybe I could be an Army helicopter pilot. That would be some adventure! Imagine me being an Army officer like my mom and dad had been. It doesn't get more adventurous than being a helicopter pilot. I wondered if I could do this and fly helicopters in the Army. Wouldn't it be something to fly and get paid for it in the U.S. Army? I would probably have to go to Vietnam if I made it through the program. I sure love flying that Cessna 150. I'll bet it would be a real thrill to fly a helicopter. Today I am going to go in there and ask them about the flight school program.

I got off the bus, walked to the recruiter's office, and opened the glass door. I asked a sergeant working there about the warrant officer flight training program. He gave me some Army recruiting materials and an aviation-related study booklet and asked me to return in a few days and take a test called the F.A.S.T. Test. The letters stood for *F*light *A*ptitude *S*tandards *T*est. I thought about that test all the way home on the bus. At home I pulled out my flight time logbook and flight materials bag. I studied the material and memorized some flight rules from my private pilot ground school materials as well. A few days later I was ready to give this my best shot.

I went back to the recruiter's office on the scheduled day. The recruiter greeted me with a firm handshake and picked up a test booklet and a pencil. An hour or so later I had finished the test, and it was sent off to be scored. I got a call a week later and was informed that I had passed and that if I wanted to go into the Army and train to be a helicopter pilot, I could enter the warrant officer training program and leave as early as the next week. The recruiter also told me that if I made it through the training, I would probably be going to Vietnam.

I went home and told my parents and family members that I was going to sign up for a great adventure. My dad listened patiently to my enthusiastic presentation and had one question for me that I still remember. He said, "You get carsick riding in the back seat of our car on the monthly trips we take to see the cousins in Tacoma. Are you sure you are ready for this?" I assured him I was and said I hadn't gotten sick during the fixed-wing flight instruction and solo so maybe those experiences were behind me.

I gave notice at my work at the jacket factory, put my car up for sale, and said my goodbyes. The next week I left for basic training at Fort Polk, Louisiana. I knew if I made it through the training, I was going to Vietnam. I was a 20-year-old young man looking for adventure. I don't remember thinking at all about the fact that I might have to kill someone as a pilot of a helicopter. I do remember knowing that the war was about saving the world from Communism. And of course, I had heard President Kennedy's challenge: "Ask not what your country can do for you. Ask what you can do for your country." That sounded like the kind of challenge I needed in my life!

Making Choices

It seemed as if a thousand suns filled the sky but yesterday
While I was walking through confusion
on the path so worn away
From far ahead out of the black
came suddenly, a shade of gray.
All the leaves that presently
were held beneath my feet
seemed black and moldy
worthless treasures, too soon to be dead.
The path's a little clearer now
Most leaves are fading fast
But some still cling to muddy shoes and bog them down till time is past.

3

Basic Infantry Training

When I enlisted in the Army, they in-processed us in an old industrial-looking building on the waterfront in Seattle. We stood in lines while teams of medical personnel poked and prodded us, weighed us, checked our height, administered hearing and vision tests, drew blood and urine, interviewed us, and generally checked out our reflexes and balance, etc. A couple of days later, we showed up at the recruiters' storefront where the recruiter swore us in. It was the first time I raised my hand and pledged formally to defend my country. The recruiter shook our hands and directed us to a van out in front for a trip to Seattle-Tacoma Airport.

They gave us a ticket from Sea-Tac Airport to Houston, Texas, on a commercial airline. As I recall, there were eight to 10 of us from the Northwest on that flight. When we got off the plane in Houston, I could hardly breathe with the humidity there. It felt like the air was stuck in my throat and I wasn't going to be able to catch my breath. You could almost cut it with a knife. There were lots of young men in the Houston airport looking like they were going off to serve in the military. It was obviously a hub for flights across the United States connecting with flights to military training bases in the South and on the East Coast.

In Houston we boarded a DC-3 for the flight to Fort Polk, Louisiana. This flight was mostly enlistees. Many had signed up to go to helicopter flight school after basic and advanced infantry training. Some of the local Southern boys called this "Treetop Airlines" because the aircraft was a non-pressurized, propeller-driven, twin-engine workhorse that flew at a little over 160 miles an hour and at a much lower altitude than the pressurized airliners of today. The trip from Texas to Louisiana was at less than 10,000 feet and went right through a number of thunderstorms, rain showers, and clouds along the route. Many of the passengers on that flight got sick, which was both a humbling and embarrassing episode for young warriors presuming to be on their way to becoming courageous helicopter pilots in Vietnam. On the flight down from Seattle to Houston, the air was electric with rumors and stories of where we were going. Comments flew

33

about like: "Fort Polk is at the end of the world. Some people call it Fort Puke. We are going to the toughest place in the U.S. Army for basic training because they want to find out if we can hack it or not." Apparently, this was going to be the first step in becoming a helicopter pilot: surviving Fort Polk, Louisiana.

I managed to keep from getting sick, just barely, but I'm glad the flight didn't go much longer because it felt like we hit every bump in the air and opportunity for turbulence between Houston, Texas, and Louisiana. We wobbled out of the plane looking like sailors coming off a three-day bender and staggered onto buses for the rest of the trip into the fort. The fort was old and gray with row upon row of World War II-type barracks that all looked the same. We first noticed the manicured grass and red mud gardens outlined with rocks around the barracks. There were polished copper pipes in the bathrooms. Two rows of bunk beds lined each barracks.

As we got off the buses, we were ordered to a parade field and lined up to be addressed by a senior post officer. We were introduced to our company commander and the drill sergeants who were to be in charge of each barracks in the company. I had come from the Pacific Northwest, and neither the neighborhood I grew up in in Seattle nor the seminary I attended had a great deal of ethnic diversity. The recruits I was now with were a cross section of America. The military was from the start a new experience in ethnic and cultural diversity for me. Most of the drill sergeants were big, tough, very direct, and very mean-looking, and they weren't smiling at any of us. And they looked like they ate broken glass for breakfast. This was not a good sign for what was ahead. They greeted us with a great big smile and an over-emphasized "Welcome to Fort Polk, Louisiana" that sounded like we were going straight to hell, no stopping, do not pass go, no free passes, no back talk, no changing your mind, and nobody cares what you think about what's going to happen to you. In fact, no one cares whether you live or die here. You signed a piece of paper, took an oath, and this is the training you are in for. They were yelling orders and they weren't waiting for anybody to mosey along to the next stopping point. They immediately taught everyone how to space themselves from the person to the side of them, in front, and behind, and said we would be marching with our gear everywhere. First, we would get some clothing issued. Then we would go to our barracks where we would be assigned our living quarters, a metal bunk, a mattress, a metal stand-up locker, and a wooden footlocker for our belongings.

The big, tough sergeant said, "Start off on your left foot. When I say 'forward march,' your left, right, left ... your left, right, left!"

"Left left left, right, left."

"Now say this after me in a loud voice," said the lean, lanky, and impeccably uniformed sergeant, "and say it all together line by line."

> Dress it right and cover down (Dress it right and cover down)
> Forty inches all around (Forty inches all around) *Louder!*
> Am I right or wrong? (You're RIGHT!)
> Am I right or wrong? (You're RIGHT!)
> Sound Off (one, two)
> Sound Off (three, four)
> That's the Fort Polk Boogie (That's the Fort Polk Boogie)
> What a crazy sound (What a crazy sound)
> *I Can't Hear You!*

We were marched from the bus offloading area to a gray wooden World War II barracks and were instructed to stand in formation and told that we would be greeted by the company commander prior to entering our assigned barracks. While we were waiting, the drill sergeants taught us how to stand at attention and how to stand at parade rest. "Attention" consisted of standing up straight and tall with your fingers curled up slightly and your thumb along the seam of your pants. Your feet were to be at a 45-degree angle forming a "V" with the heels of your shoes touching and your feet forming the sides of the "V." Your eyes were to be looking straight forward with your chin in and your chest out.

The position of "Parade Rest" was taken by moving your left leg out about shoulder width and placing your hands together in the small of your back with the left-hand palm cupped against your belt and the right hand over the left. These two commands would become important to be used in the presence of the company commander, or any other officer, and/or a drill sergeant. "At ease" was another less formal command for parade rest. The command "fall out" meant you could leave the formation to walk (but mostly you were expected to run) somewhere, everywhere, anywhere … particularly when in a company or platoon formation. "Fall out" in practice was often given during a break from formation and was often accompanied by "Smoke 'em if you've got 'em!" This statement had little significance for me other than to signal at least a few minutes of rest without fear of interruption. Senior Sergeant Bacon, who called us to attention, introduced Captain Miller, our company commander. The officers in Training Company E were Captain Miller, 2nd Lt. Terrible (not kidding), and 2nd Lt. Doczy. Of course, a lowly trainee would seldom if ever talk to or even see these men. There were 222 trainees in Company E, and we were divided into four platoons.

The sergeants in our Second Platoon were Drill Sergeant Wilder, Drill Sergeant Scoville, Drill Sergeant Weissbohn, and Drill Sergeant Calderin. I was in the Second Platoon, Company E, First Battalion, First Training

Brigade. This was a busy time for training recruits, and we had more than the usual number in each platoon and in our company.

That night we went to dinner in the mess hall. In line, we were told to stand at attention and advance one person at a time until there was a space for us in the mess hall to eat. I made the mistake of addressing a lieutenant supervising the mess hall as "Lieutenant" since I recognized his rank and I was a sort of gregarious person. At this faux pas, the drill sergeant came over, got in my face, and came totally unglued. "This is an officer. You don't even talk to an officer unless you have a very important reason to do so and then you call him 'sir'! Is that clear, trainee? Now drop down here in the mess hall and give me 25 pushups and don't you ever make that mistake again on my watch. If you want something you talk to me, trainee! I am your drill sergeant. I am the only one here who really loves you. I care about your sorry ass. Who will you come to with your sorry-ass problems, trainee? That's right, your favorite drill sergeant, Sergeant Wilder. I am here to help you … and you obviously need a lot of help! And I am going to do my best to give it to you."

From Fort Polk, Louisiana
Jan 9, 1967

Dear Mom and Dad,

One week out of the way but somehow it seems like a month. We took a physical training test when we arrived and I did well. There were obstacle courses and low crawling under barbed wire. I ran the mile and did calisthenics and marching and running in full packs. Classes we have attended are in military courtesy, justice, and marching moves. I have the sorest feet in the world and many aches and pains but I should get toughened up by the end of next week. We were issued an M-14 rifle.

We had a class on dismantling it and were told it would be our most important tool and friend as a soldier…. I got some shots, eight altogether now, but we are just starting according to what they say. I was waiting in mess hall on cadre the other day and addressed Lieutenant as Lieutenant not Sir—lucky to escape with my hide my ears still ringing from the lesson.

Love,
Your Son, Fred

*   *   *

We had worked hard for about a month of training and were beginning to gel and develop as a hard-charging barracks of recruits. We'd been through marching with packs, the rifle range, classes on military protocol, regular inspections of our barracks, learning to eat square meals in the mess hall with military manners, how to polish the floors to a shine, keep our gear organized, and shine those brass water pipes under the sinks to a mirror finish.

The climate in Louisiana was alternately hot and humid and cold and wet. The "modus operandi" for a hike was that you started out often in a rain shower with your rubberized poncho in your pack and were not allowed to put it on until instructed to do so by your drill instructor. I'm not saying that our drill instructors were sadistic or unreasonable, but it was fascinating to us that when the clouds inevitably parted and the sun came out we were instructed to put on our ponchos. This covering soon turned into a personal sauna as the sun got brighter and the hike got longer. Then as the rain came again, we would be instructed to put our ponchos back in the pack to return to hiking in the rain and getting soaked. If someone got fatigued or fell during the hike, the remaining troops were encouraged to walk right over him with the drill instructor yelling at them. All of this, we speculated, was designed to toughen us up and prepare us for the jungles of Vietnam and the dual seasons of the dry, hot weather and the torrential rains of the monsoon season.

We learned to play the game. We also learned there was the right way, the wrong way, and the Army way. Each day was filled with something new to learn. There were many chances to push our physical endurance to the limit and regular opportunities for being caught doing things wrong. We also found out that when we worked hard together we were able to accomplish far more than we would ever have chosen to do as individuals. When one person messed up, everyone paid for the mistake, by doing extra push-ups or running extra distances.

The drill instructors seemed to enjoy their work way too much, particularly if it involved trainee discomfort. Gradually we saw our endurance increase and were stretched at every turn to run one more mile or do 10 more pushups. We gradually got in the best physical shape of our lives and learned to work together in a way that most of us had never experienced before.

From Fort Polk, Louisiana
Sunday, January 22, 1967

Dear Mom and Dad,

Just back from 9 o'clock Mass on a cloudy windy Sunday morning. Bivouac took place from Monday to Thursday last week. Temperatures were near freezing and between the mud and the cold we were all very glad to get back to a warm barracks and clean clothes. We also appreciate the food a little more after 4 days of C rations. The final night of bivouac went through the infiltration course. This consisted of crawling over logs, under barbed wire, and through thick mud under live machine gun fire 44" off the ground and occasional blasts of TNT from deep sand bagged demolition pits. We also were trained in close combat methods advancing down range in teams with live ammo on targets. Well only two weeks to go and we'll all really be glad when it's over. No leave or passes are in sight.... Next Saturday is final physical fitness test then tests on drill, 1st aid, guard duty, and military courtesy.... Graduation day will be on Friday, February 24th.... Will need to buy 6 more sets of fatigues because at flight school need a clean starched pair every morning. That should hit me for about $30 and leave me about $30. Not much new going to show this afternoon. So long for this week.

Love,
Your Son,
Fred

One day as we returned to our barracks after a rather grueling 10-mile hike, we all took showers and were resting in our bunks after dinner when a surprisingly upbeat Sergeant Wilder was praising our efforts on the challenging hike, singing our praises in relation to the other adjacent barracks, and suggesting that we might have earned the right to a little social celebration at a nearby mini PX (post exchange). Of course, we all were spring-loaded to believe that we had really earned this little celebration and enthusiastically agreed that it would be a fitting reward for our efforts to go to the local PX/mini mart for some refreshment. Some of the savvier members of our unit were a little skeptical that Sergeant Wilder was really sincere about us earning this reward. However, everyone got into the spirit and we all walked down the street casually together in small groups for whatever we were about to experience. It felt strangely civilian and relaxing to not be marching on post. There were a few tables outside, and the drill instructor seemed to know the attractive attendant at the counter from previous visits.

In Louisiana at the time, young people could drink what was called 3.2 beer if they were 18 years old. Sergeant Wilder encouraged everyone to have a few beers, and after our hard day of marching we were more than ready to do so. He joined in, smiling all the while, though he didn't attempt to keep up with the recruits but just nursed his own one beer while most of the trainees all had three or four each; some even had a few more. Sergeant Wilder really seemed to enjoy the camaraderie, and after an hour and a half it was dark and he led the group back to our barracks to retire for the evening. There was lots of talking and good-natured interaction and we had lights out promptly at 10:00 p.m.

At 3:00 a.m. the next day, the lights came on and Sergeant Wilder had reverted back to his previous persona. "Everybody up! We are going on a march!"

Groans arose from many bunks, but the sergeant only became more animated. We were directed to put on our packs and fall out on the street in front of the barracks in formation. "Let's go, move it, move it, move it. Let's get going! No laggards here!"

Sergeant Wilder had the same smile on that he had at the mini mart. "Forward march!" started us out, and after a block "Double time march!" took the pace up a couple of notches. Guys started stumbling and then collapsing from the rigor and the effects of the previous night's celebration, and began falling by the wayside.

"If anyone falls down, I want you to just step over him" was the advice being shouted at us by our training sergeant. This provided additional motivation to stay in line. As we completed the approximately five-mile, double-time march, we had lost about 10 percent of the platoon, and some of those guys lost their cookies along the way. We now knew one reason why the place was sometimes called "Fort Puke." "Never trust a drill sergeant who is smiling" became a mantra for our barracks.

Fort Polk soon became our familiar temporary home. We gradually learned the ropes, from the initial very short haircut and ill-fitting uniforms to the institutional food and the ever-appropriate military advice: "Never volunteer!" We learned this in spades through an experience in which we were asked if any of us had attended college. Those who eagerly raised their hands found out that a few college boys were needed to peel hundreds of potatoes and clean out the grease traps at the mess hall.

> From Fort Polk, Louisiana
> Sunday, January 28, 1967

Dear Mom and Dad,

... took my final physical fitness test this morning and did well. Got another pass for this weekend but I am staying on post to save money. Graduation is next Friday, then we will probably be held over for another 8 days until our report date at Fort Wolters on March 4. Really appreciated your last letter, got it on bivouac. Weather was really cold & wet. Now sun is out and promises to be a clear but cool day.... Next month and ½ will be concentrated harassment. I will keep you posted but may be short of time once in a while so excuse me if letters don't arrive every week.

> Love,
> Your son, Fred

> From Charleston Hotel,
> Lake Charles, Louisiana
> Sunday, February 5, 1967

Dear Mom and Dad,

...I'm on a two-day pass because all of those who qualified expert or sharpshooter with their weapon were given the opportunity. I was very worried about qualifying ... my practice scores all week were pretty low. On qualifying day I shot sharpshooter, which is in the middle between marksman and expert. I was very happy and proud and will get that particular medal at the end of training.

...I'm in Lake Charles with seven other sharpshooters. The bells in the Church tower just tolled for 8:30 Mass and as I look out the window of our room Lake Charles is a calm, glassy mirror, a very beautiful sight. Very different and some white mansions along the way, interspersed with rolling plains and green fields all seemed so different and refreshing.

Last week ... marching at a killing pace 5 miles to the range in full gear then running 2 of the miles on the way back. Our spirits are high and we have real pride in being in the toughest and the best company ... in the fort since July 1966.

Last night we went to a few bars and had a few beers. Bill got thrown out of one because he was colored.... Bill took it well, he plays it cool and is so used to it, so we laughed it off and left. Next week gas chamber and hand to hand combat.

Love,
Your Son,
Fred

*   *   *

As we completed our Basic and Advanced Infantry Training and were looking forward to leaving Fort Polk and going on to Fort Wolters, Texas, for Warrant Officer Candidate School and primary flight training, our barracks was informed that we would be in a two-week "holdover" status before our class of helicopter pilots and warrant officer candidates would be ready to begin. Rather than have us just wait around for two weeks in the notorious bars around Leesville, it was decided by higher authority that we needed to be productive. We would receive some value-added escape and evasion training. We also would be harvesting palmetto leaves in the swamps to create simulated Viet Cong villages for use in the training command at Fort Polk. Our destination would be Opelousas, Louisiana, where the friendly wildlife, we were told, consisted of alligators, water moccasins, poisonous spiders, and armadillos. We would sleep in tents at night and harvest palmetto during the day to be loaded into trucks and taken back to Fort Polk.

We rode in the back of deuce-and-a-half trucks under canvas canopies for the trip through the bayous and swamps of Louisiana to our jungle destination. When we arrived, we set up camp and an outdoor mess hall and set about our assigned tasks. About the third day in the swamp, as the afternoon turned into evening, a couple of dump trucks arrived and, to everyone's pleasant surprise, it turned out that they were loaded with 3.2 beer. The trucks made a circle and backed up; then their beds started rising up and they unloaded their pallets with cases of beer onto the boggy floor of the swamp. Eager trainees were given the go-ahead sign by the sergeants in charge and began opening the cases, and a good time was had by all. After everyone was adequately "tuned up," a few of the local Southern boys demonstrated their best impression of redneck rodeo by catching and riding some of the armadillos around the camp area. We must have scared off the alligators, for none were seen. But as we peeled off the bark from some of the palm trees there were shouts of excitement when a few water moccasins were exposed.

In the swamp we were introduced to camping, Army style. A large canvas tent served as the mess hall, and garbage cans were filled with water and heated with gas-fired stainless steel heaters to scalding hot temperature for washing the aluminum compartmentalized trays that some of our food was served in. A latrine area was established with trenches dug and some canvas screening that developed quite an ambiance before the multi-day assignment was over. We also had some meals of C-rations, and we learned to use a P-38 Army-issued can opener to release the contents of each can of prepared food. We learned that some of the meals were borderline edible and others were not. Later in Vietnam these meals became a regular part of our missions and, when heated with a small amount of JP-4 jet fuel drained into a C-ration can, became epicurean delights, sort of. Our tents seemed to keep us from the rumored snakes, alligators, and spiders, and the beer tasted awfully good after a hard day's work cutting palmetto fronds in the swamps of Opelousas, Louisiana. This experience was definitely a highlight in the join-the-Army-see-the-world category.

From Fort Polk, Louisiana
Sunday, February 12, 1967

Dear Dad and Mom,

...glad to hear that you got my letter.... Last week was crammed with training, running to every class and exercise, night fire at targets after dark, gas chamber (from which my eyes are still watering), hand to hand combat, lots of "Army drill #1" calisthenics and threw grenades.

Next week will be bivouac. We're all hoping for good weather.... Everyone is anxious for the next 3 weeks to get over so we can get out of this red mud they call a Fort. We had an orientation the other night on the Warrant Officer Program. It sounds like 5 months at Ft. Wolters, Texas (60 miles from Dallas) and 5 at Ft. Rucker, Alabama, with no foreseeable leaves in the near future. A lot of guys in my company are going to flight school and want to get married and are pretty upset with this no leave in the future line but I think it will work out for them....

Love,
Your Son, Fred

4

Primary and Advanced Helicopter Flight Training

Fort Wolters was located in the town of Mineral Wells, Texas, about 40 miles west of Fort Worth. An impressive welcome to the adventure of learning to fly helicopters in the U.S. Army greeted us as we entered the main gate. The archway over the entrance road was guarded on either side by a helicopter. One was a Hughes TH55 and the other was a Hiller OH23. These were the two trainer aircraft choices of the Army. We would be assigned one of these types for the duration of our primary flight training and would become intimately familiar with its unique characteristics and challenges.

The program we were about to enter was formally called the WOR-WAC program (Warrant Officer Rotary Wing Aviation Course). There was a parallel course conducted for commissioned officers called the ORWAC course (Officer Rotary Wing Aviation Course). Regular officers were accorded additional privileges. Warrant officer candidates were the recipients of the dual gifts of mentoring and harassment from TAC officers, who were themselves combat veterans.

Fort Wolters had the largest heliport in the world with about 1,200 helicopters located down the main road a ways and south of the fort. Our company was the First WOC Company. There were four sections in the company and ours was A-4. There were 44 of us in the section. We wore red baseball-type caps, and our section lead TAC officer was Mr. M.

From Fort Wolters, Texas
Sunday, March 5, 1967

Dear Mom and Dad,

...before I left Fort Polk, I was put on a three-day detail. We went into the Louisiana swamps in a place called Opelousas to cut a palm-like plant called palmetto. They use it in mock VC villages for advanced infantry training here. I got back tired and dirty, saw a water moccasin poisonous snake and some armadillos ... ever since getting off the bus it's "candidate this" and "candidate that." We eat at attention, with our knife fork and spoon in a special place.... We must ask in a prescribed manner to be excused,

42

then they excuse us in a group and in a prescribed manner before we can leave. We live in a dorm-type set up but our barracks are broken up into cubicles with 2 candidates to a cubicle. We spit shine the floor with wax and I am very busy keeping my boots and brass in appropriate order.... We must salute every officer we meet and greet them appropriately such as "Sir, Candidate McCarthy, Good Evening Sir." Then we wait for him to return the salute.... We wear brass on our fatigues and uniforms that says WOC (Warrant Officer Candidate). The chain of command changes every week, so we could end up as a platoon sergeant or a squad leader at any time. Everyone must demonstrate leadership when given such authority. All are graded on the ability to lead. I now have nine full sets of fatigues and am supposed to break starch in fatigues every day.

> Love,
> Your Son,
> Fred

The helicopters for instructional purposes of our company would be TH-55s that were called the Mattel Messerschmitt. They looked and sounded like a high-pitched toy compared to the larger Hueys and Bells. In flight they sounded like a bee when the rotor was buzzing by in the air at flight RPM. The length of our training at Fort Wolters was a little over four months. The first four weeks were called preflight and consisted of classroom instruction, physical training, inspections, study halls, and learning about becoming a warrant officer in the United States Army.

The bugle blew each day at 5:00 a.m. and we had to hit the ground running to get dressed, shaved, showered, prepare our area for display and fall out of the barracks within about 15 minutes, standing at attention in front of our TAC officer. We marched everywhere: to the mess hall, to supply for uniforms and flight equipment, to the barber for haircuts, and to the mess hall for meals. The marching started off as forward march but inevitably changed to "double time ... march" which was a sort of shuffle/jog along to the next destination.

We ate our meals in a very regimented fashion designed to build a sense of team spirit. We went through a line with metal trays extended for the cooks to put heaping portions of food on them; then we proceeded to a table where we stood at attention, holding our trays by the next open chair, until all seats were filled; and then the last arrival would say, "Ready ... seats," and we would all sit in unison. I recalled that my father had described his experience in ROTC as having to eat what he called square meals where you lifted the utensil up in the air vertically and then brought it in to your mouth horizontally. This was the way we were expected to eat as well. Sitting up straight with dignity and decorum, we ate our meal and waited until the last person at the table was finished, and then a command was given—"Ready ... up"—and everyone would rise and then proceed to place our empty trays on a moving rack going back into the kitchen area for cleaning.

Our living quarters were in concrete block buildings with polished concrete floors. We were assigned two to a room. Inspections occurred each morning and evening for most of preflight. Frequently during the day, we would come back to the barracks from classes and find that our belongings were thrown all over the place and the demerits were listed on a checklist at our bunk. The items checked each day were our bunks being tight enough to bounce a coin on them, our brass shined inside and out, our extra boots shined, our shirts lined up with equal spacing of the hangers, the books ordered from larger to smaller on our desk, the gear in our locker neatly arranged, no half-completed letters in the desk drawer, the chair and desk in a straight line, etc. I believe the TAC officers watched for certain individuals, and I ended up being one of them. I ended up accumulating so many demerits that I went for two months without a weekend off. Most of the other WOCs in my flight were issued passes at the end of preflight, while I marched taxi time by myself in front of the barracks. This consisted of marching by myself back and forth on the sidewalk adjacent to our barracks for hours and calling out "about face" at each turn, "forward march" for each segment, and "halt" at the end of the walkway.

Ultimately, I was called before the company commander for excessive demerits and asked if I wanted to quit. I said emphatically, "Sir, Candidate McCarthy, no sir!"

And so the commander said he would give me one more chance and put me in charge of the flight for marching purposes. This turned out to be my saving grace. I have a loud voice and liked to call cadence and make up funny verses, so the men enjoyed marching when I was calling the cadence. I concluded this must have bothered our TAC officer at first because, when we marched by him dressed impeccably in his chrome helmet, bloused combat boots, and swagger stick, he would glare at me with a look of disgust on his face. After a while it began to look like he was somewhat amused by the comradery it engendered, and he would seem to acknowledge that it built up esprit de corps among the men and made the blocks pass quickly as we made it to our next destination. Of course, he never commented that I was doing a good job. Positive affirmation wasn't in his vocabulary as a TAC officer at this point in our training. Here are a few examples of the kind of cadence I would call:

> I don't know about today. Rain is causing some dismay.
> When we all get good and wet. Our poncho they'll let us get.
> I don't know but I've been told. Mr. M is really cold.
> He enjoys demerit giving. What a way to make a living.
> Am I right or wrong? Tell me if I'm wrong!
> Sound off one two, sound off three four
> cadence count one, two three four, one two, three four.

Let's all give a great big shout. Let's all really work it out
Taxi time is so much fun. That's why we all get a ton
Jody is back home you know. Taking your girl to a show.
He is having a big time. While we're marching here in line.
Am I right or wrong? Tell me if I'm wrong!
Sound off one two, sound off three four
Cadence count one, two three four, One two, three four.

From Fort Wolters, Texas
Sunday, March 12, 1967

Dear Mom and Dad,

...90 degrees yesterday and hot.... I know it will be hotter than hell this afternoon. If this is March I bet this place is a furnace in the Summer. I've been going to classes all week long in leadership, map reading, general qualities of an officer, military justice and military law. We are up in the morning at five and ... out in formation after my bed is made and all my gear is straight in only fifteen minutes. Classes start at 7:00am to 11:30am then also go from 1:00pm to 4:30pm. After this we have physical training for 45 minutes. We go to evening mess and return back to our barracks, and straighten what we can of our gear and area. Then ... a one-hour study period at night and another one hour in silence to work on personal gear. After all this we work together on the billets for 30 minutes and lights out is at 10:00pm. The discipline, attention in ranks, and silence, and etiquette at meals are coming second nature now. We double-time everywhere we go. We have a party at the end of preflight in 3 weeks and are all looking forward to it. They have it in large downtown hotel ballroom in Mineral Wells and invite girls from the sororities at a girls' college from nearby Denton, Texas ... the harassment is so we will pay particular attention to the smallest of details because in aviation one small slip can cost you your life. One candidate sitting across from me at mess had his hand on the table and the tactical officer gave him 2 hrs of drill to march on Saturday or Sunday....

Love,
Your son,
Fred

I was the fifth in our flight to solo the TH55, probably just a fluke of nature, but it was sufficient to show that I was serious about completing this challenging phase and ultimately becoming an Army aviator. Some parts of flight training were particularly difficult, like learning to hover. When the instructor first demonstrates this, it looks so easy. Then when he turns the controls over to you, the aircraft quickly gets out of control and is rescued by the instructor who lets you know in no uncertain terms what an uncoordinated jerk you are and how you are putting his life at risk each time he gives you the controls. After about seven to 10 hours of instruction, the coordination of the controls, which seems like it will never come, magically comes together for most people. Some individuals really struggle with this. It was a point at which some students washed out of the program. So there was a make-it-or-break-it dimension to learning this primary maneuver.

Another challenging but very important part of helicopter flight training is to master the autorotation. This is a maneuver associated with a simulated engine failure. The collective is lowered, and the pitch is reduced
in the rotor blades, and the helicopter descends with the air rushing up
through the blades with the inertia of the rapidly descending aircraft keeping the blades turning. As the helicopter approaches the ground, the pilot
flares the aircraft back with a move of the cyclic control and cushions the
aircraft onto the ground with the collective control. It all has to be done
with great timing and application of control force, and when done just right
results in the helicopter settling to the ground without power and without damage to its components. The pulling of pitch has to be timed exactly.
Too early and you would fall the last few feet to the runway. Too late and
you would slam into the runway. Flight instructors really earned their pay
teaching this high-stakes maneuver. I was personally appreciative of the
extent of this training later, as I experienced two engine failures and autorotations in Vietnam.

Our flight training at Fort Wolters was divided into phases. We
had one set of instructors for the first phase and another for the second.
It was exciting moving from basic controls in flying straight and level to
doing turns, climbs and descents, day flying and night flying, local area
and cross-country flying both dual and solo. One instructor was very
high-strung and uptight, and the other was very laid back and grandfa-
therly in his instruction. We wore our flight suits for flight instruction
and rode in buses from the fort either to the main heliport or to a staging
field. While one group was up flying another would be in the bus or a small
building studying their flight subject lessons. Then the candidates who flew
out to the stage field would adjourn to the bus or building while they were
replaced in the cockpit by the next student. When a student soloed, the bus
back to the fort made a stop at a local hotel that had an outside entrance
to the swimming pool, and there was a ceremonious process that involved
throwing the successful solo student high up in the air and into the pool
after a raucous countdown to blastoff.

Two men had a profound effect on my success in flight school when
I was in jeopardy and at a particularly teachable moment, and their influence was significant in my life. One was named Jim Lucking. The other
was named Bob (Jim) McCarthy. Each was an experienced sergeant when
accepted into the Warrant Officer Candidate Program. They both made
a personal choice to enter the program after a few years of experience in
the Army, had attained the rank of sergeant, and had backgrounds that
included knowing the ropes and implementing military procedures, discipline, and attention to detail that only comes with that kind of experience.

I can vividly remember a spring day in the First Warrant Officer

Candidate company barracks of the Red Hats at Fort Wolters when we were in our concrete block company building with its spit-shined concrete floors and meticulously clean spartan surroundings. We were reviewing the previous week's activities in this first phase of our training that was called pre-flight. This period of time included daily inspections and harassment by TAC officers, marching and double timing, calisthenics, and classes on post procedures and military protocols.

Jim McCarthy led off the questions with, "Mac, how do you think it's going?"

My response was, "Not too well! I don't know why, but this TAC officer really has it in for me. I think I am getting more demerits than anyone else in the barracks."

Jim Lucking said, "Yes you are. When they get your number, they will ride your ass and try to throw you out of here. Don't let them get to you. Would you like some advice?"

"Yes, I can use all of the help I can get at this point," I replied.

Jim looked out the window and then began with some questions: "How many pairs of boots do you have? How many belt buckles? How many sets of brass? The key is to have a set of spit-shined boots and a highly polished belt buckle and set of brass insignias … that you never wear! You're gonna have to part with some of your money. You get this stuff highly shined and set it aside for display. You take out every one of your uniforms and go over them with a fine-toothed comb to find any lanyards [hanging threads] and you cut or burn them off. If they find that kind of thing, they will be all over you. If you have your gear organized and straight, they will not mess with you but will move on to someone else."

I had already formed a negative relationship with our TAC officer, who I began to believe saw me as young and unaware of the details that were involved in keeping my uniform and belongings in inspection-ready condition. This had already resulted in an inordinate number of accumulating demerits and daily destruction of my area, locker and belongings by the TAC staff while I was attending class or physical training. As the days passed fewer bunks or locker areas were disturbed. However, when we would return to the barracks, my gear and that of a few other candidates was thrown all over the barracks.

I was painfully aware of the TAC staff's dissatisfaction with my performance since it was reinforced for me on a regular basis in the following manner. When a TAC officer came down the hall, we were expected to brace—this meant standing up against the wall at attention with feet locked and eyes straight ahead—and in a strong clear voice state, "Sir, Candidate McCarthy, good afternoon, sir!"

This was usually for me just the beginning of a painful daily exchange that was characterized by all sorts of questions that had no right answer. The TAC officer would get his face two inches from my face and respond: "Candidate McCarthy, it sounds like you are very confused. Do you really believe you can become a warrant officer and be entrusted with commanding an expensive helicopter for the U.S. Army?"

Any attempts at apology or explanation had to be preceded by "Sir, Candidate McCarthy…" and followed by "…Sir, Candidate McCarthy, thank you, sir."

Our TAC officer seemed to get energized by my inevitable mistakes and stumbling misstatements of the required scripted responses. The TAC officer would respond, "Don't thank me, candidate. Learn to do things right and pay attention to detail. I don't know what kind of screening process the Army has now, but it definitely failed when you were let in. You are the sorriest excuse for a warrant officer candidate that we have ever seen. Our job is to get rid of people like you before you kill someone because you haven't paid attention to the details. We can't let an idiot be entrusted with an expensive Army helicopter, can we Candidate McCarthy?"

"Sir, Candidate McCarthy, no sir!" was my reply.

"Why no, we can't. So maybe we should throw your sorry ass out of here right now. Would that be doing you a favor, Candidate McCarthy? Would you like to be thrown out of here and be an enlisted man for the rest of your tour?"

"Sir, Candidate McCarthy, no sir, I want to succeed here and learn to be an Army aviator."

"Then we will see whether you can hack it, Candidate McCarthy! You have a long way to go!"

The next day, I was summoned to come into the inner sanctum that was the office of our TAC officers. Three of them were present. Two were standing at parade rest. The third was seated behind an official-looking desk. I came in and stood at attention against the back wall and addressed the head TAC officer behind the desk. "Sir, Candidate McCarthy, reporting, sir."

"At ease Candidate McCarthy!" was the unexpected response. "We have been talking about the sorry state of your military bearing and the many demerits you have accumulated in the short time you have been here, and we have come to one conclusion. It's sink-or-swim time for you. We are going to give you a chance to prove that you really want to be here and can cut it here. Do you have any idea what we are talking about Candidate McCarthy?"

"Sir, Candidate McCarthy, yes sir!"

"Well then, what is it that we are going to do, Candidate McCarthy?"

"Sir, Candidate McCarthy, I don't know what it is, sir!"

"Well, you are in luck because we are gathered here to tell you the answer you are looking for. We are going to put you in charge of the whole company, Candidate McCarthy. You can't even take care of your own area. How do you think you will do if you are in charge of the whole damn company?"

"Sir, Candidate McCarthy, I will lead the company, sir!"

"Well, Candidate McCarthy, that will be a real show. We can't wait to see how you screw this one up, and when we do, we are going to throw your sorry ass out of here. Do you understand what we are saying Candidate McCarthy?"

"Sir, Candidate McCarthy, yes sir, I understand!"

"Candidate, you are dismissed."

"Sir, Candidate McCarthy, yes sir!" I saluted, turned about face, and left the company officers' room.

As I walked back to our cubicle I thought to myself, "Well, at least all of the cards are on the table." The TAC officer has not only got my number in spades but he has also co-opted the other TAC officers and the leadership into a joint effort to push me and see what I can take. This is no time to buckle under the pressure. Maybe I come across too timid, too disorganized, not serious enough about keeping my area highly organized, and not attentive enough to minute details and military protocols. I will show them.

I am going to organize my area and look for every little speck of dust. My brass and boots will shine enough to see my face in them. All of my clothes and uniform parts will be folded exactly right and placed on display like I live in a museum. I will keep a positive attitude, control my voice, lower the pitch in my voice, and give it right back to them. I know I have made friends in the company and they will back me up! I have the capability of projecting a loud voice, and I will use it when I am in front leading the company to convey to other candidates and the TAC officers that there is no question about who is leading the company and what the expectations are for high performance and compliance. I can do this. Game on!

A Friend

A friend is one who senses things
that also make sense to me.
Who sees the flow of life
and loves its every turn and bending spree.
Who takes the time to hear the words of children
pure and simple, crying for
the seeds of truth.
The lenses that they need to see their place on life's enormous tree.
In whom I find a love of life to be
And know he sees it too, in me.

Fort Wolters, Texas
Tuesday, March 21, 1967

Dear Nan,

    …I was writing a letter to cousin Jerry but during inspection a TAC officer found it (We're not supposed to have ½ written letters around, either write all at once or tear them up, can't have anything ½ done letters lying around. Pretty crazy huh?) I got demerits for it and he wrote all over it so I just threw it away…. I got a pass from Sat noon till 6 o'clock Easter but I had 11 military letters to write & lots to study for final map test. Passed the test today and all is well. Looking forward to party Friday night & transfer up to the flight line on Saturday. Sent home for some civilian clothes in a week will be able to wear them if we get passes, which I probably won't get for a while judging from my past demerits. There is always a ray of hope. Weather is in the high 70s and comfortable. The outlook is for intermittent harassment.

    Thanks again for cookies.

Love,
Your grandson,
Fred

Giving It All

On lightened day of mild degree
My venture led me to the sea
Where at her feet my thoughts flowed free
I asked her what she thought of me.
My eyes were down,
her arm drew back
And left a stone half white, half black
Be all of what you try to be
Keep not half back she said to me.

From Fort Wolters, Texas
Easter Sunday, March 26, 1967

Dear Mom and Dad,

    It's Sunday night and I have to study for a map final test tomorrow…. Last night I saw a show and had few drinks at the NCO club. We've been having final tests this last week and so far I have done well enough but tomorrow will be a tough one. The weather has been relatively moderate in temp but yesterday we had lightening and a hailstorm. I saw Paul Fleming. He is a senior graduating next week and going on to Alabama. He gave me a few tips and pointers. Only 215 out of 425 originals in his class made it as far as he has. Don McNeil, Kevin's friend, strangely enough, lives in the same barracks as me and seems to be a real nice guy … the same old harassment and getting ridden all of the time. It bugs a lot of guys but they're going to have to chain me up and throw me out of here before I would quit. I just say the hell with it and do what they say…. I should get paid $180 for this month & might start looking for some transportation. It all depends on what the pass future looks like and how I progress when we go to the flight line….

Love,
Your Son, Fred

From Fort Wolters, Texas
Sunday, April 16, 1967

Dear Mom and Dad,

...I soloed yesterday number 5 in my flight.... I haven't had any passes yet because of demerits. In fact, I've been walking taxi time and details every weekend. Our TAC officer seems to have nailed me as the proverbial one from every flight and I have had to put up with extra inspections and so many demerits for dust and improper displays that I have already been before the captain for excessive demerits and the way it looks I will go before him again this week. I have been made the squad leader for this week.... With my early solo and, if I do well as squad leader, this will reflect well on my rating.... A windstorm hit the heliport and totaled out 60 machines, extensively damaging 150 so our time on the flight line has increased to compensate for the downed aircraft.... In all of the rush I am finding myself more organized and responsible. Things must be done here in order of importance, and they must be accomplished thoroughly, completely, and quickly. I can notice a definite increase in my responsibility and I have always kept a positive attitude and drive so these demerit problems ought to come around and things should start falling into place soon.

Love
Your Son,
Fred

Fort Wolters, Texas
Wednesday, May 17, 1967

Dear Mom and Dad,

...now have 50 hours of logged flying time in and I am finally getting a natural feel for the controls and ear for the right RPM sound from the engine so am beginning to appreciate the green valleys and far reaching rocky plateaus that dot the flat country around here.

Everything takes on a different perspective and a feeling of freedom from 2,000'. I got an 85% on my primary check ride. The weather has been quite moderate in the 80s but a few days approach the 95 mark and gave us a taste of what the summer will have to offer. I have completed courses in mechanics and aerodynamics, at present classes are concerned with flight planning and course navigation, using a computer similar to a slide rule and referring back to many hours of map reading we studied in preflight. Harassment is an ever-present friend and I got my first pass in 3 months last week and looks like I may get another this week if everything goes all right.

So Long For now, Love,
Your Son, Fred

Fort Wolters, Texas
Saturday, May 27, 1967

Dear Mom and Dad,

...I have about an 85% academic average ... flight instruction is far from a breeze. A great deal of coordination is required to fly a helicopter, very much more than learning to fly a fixed wing airplane. There are controls in both of your hands and pedals for both feet. We must constantly divide our attention between about 12 important instruments and the outside area … your instructor calls you a stupid fool for one hour straight over the intercom and describes how you almost killed him and yourself on that last time … glad to solo and now can go up and yell at myself…. I soloed for one hour yesterday.

…there were tornado warnings in all quadrants…. It was not too safe a feeling being up there…. It started thundering and heavy lightening began. They turned a red light on in the control tower and we all came in with no problems. That was quite an adventure. I always have all of you in my prayers. Two tornadoes touched down between here and Fort Worth last night so maybe we'll get some excitement today. I got a $10,000 life insurance policy that was approved and recommended by the post commander. It covers flying here as well as in Vietnam. Our Tactical Officer said I did a good job as squad leader so a little pressure is off. When we go out to heliport in buses I get a helicopter assigned, preflight it, and fly it out to a stage field about six miles away solo….

Love,
Your Son,
Fred

*   *   *

Primary flight training was divided into two phases at Fort Wolters, basic and advanced. In the basic phase we learned, among other skills, the maneuvers of straight and level flight, climbs, descents, turns, emergency procedures, takeoffs, landings, autorotations, and hovering. During the second phase we were taught navigation and landing on various pinnacles, slopes, and in confined areas. The Army leased land from farmers and ranchers around Mineral Wells, outside of the base. There were three types of areas designated for three levels of difficulty based on the size of the clearing, terrain type, obstacles, and height of surrounding trees or brush. Each was marked with one of three tires, which could be seen from the air, designating its level of difficulty. A white tire indicated a low level, and yellow indicated a moderate level of difficulty and required the approval of the flight instructor to enter solo. The highest level of difficulty was marked with a red tire and required that an instructor pilot be with the student.

These training areas were important because our instructors knew we would be flying into very confined and difficult areas in combat and we needed to know how to assess the risks and make the safest approaches into and departures from these types of areas. We did some of these confined area landings and takeoffs solo and some with an instructor. The procedure was quite involved. Upon landing into the wind and lined up with the longest part of the open area, we would secure the helicopter controls, leave the aircraft running and blades turning at low RPM and then jump out to examine the area. We would pace off the distance of the longest open area by walking from one end to the other. We were to take a handful of dry grass and throw it up in the air and note the direction of the wind and then carefully get back into the helicopter, buckle in our safety harness and go through a detailed pre-takeoff list. This involved making sure all of the gauges were in the green and the helicopter engine was eased up from idle to full operating RPM. Next we would bring the helicopter to a three-foot hover, carefully move it to the downwind part of the confined area, turn it around and then take off into the wind, moving from a hover into translational lift with the cyclic control, and climb out of the area by applying upward force to the collective while keeping the direction of departure in alignment with the pedals and adding just the right amount of throttle to compensate for the increased load of a climb on the engine. It was a delicate balancing act, and the skids would normally just barely clear the treetops at the departure end of the area. This process was important in that a heavily loaded helicopter doesn't just take off straight up in the air. It is moved forward deftly until the lift shifts from a hover into translational lift and forward flight. These were interesting maneuvers and done with a high degree of instructor control and oversight to ensure the safety of the pilot and the aircraft. We were taken into a white tire area and the instructor demonstrated this process. The next lesson involved us going solo into the same area. We would go with an instructor into a yellow tire area with an instructor pilot, followed by doing it solo.

When debriefing this second procedure, I mentioned that I had seen a red tire area close by and went in and out of it as well, assuming I might get extra credit. I guess I enjoyed the challenge of this type of flying and didn't hear the part about it being dangerous and requiring an instructor with us, because the instructor, who was already a bit high-strung, leapt out of his seat and was in my face and on my case once again. He took me aside and said with a great deal of intensity: "You are in big trouble here. You are not listening to the directions I give you. I am not talking just for my own health or entertainment. Is there any question in your mind about what I am telling you right now? Because if there is we have got a real problem here. If I were to tell what you have done to the captain you might be grounded and out of the program. Now get your act together, listen carefully to each and every directive I give you and don't ever again do something like this that you are not cleared to do on a flight lesson. Is that clear, Mr. McCarthy?"

"Yes sir!" was my reply from the position of attention that I found myself taking.

"Now get back to the table and let's finish debriefing confined area procedures with the other students. Are there any questions about what I have told you?"

"No sir!"

I returned to the table, and the other two students in our group were noticeably silent as our instructor resumed the lesson, but the redness in his face remained during the debriefing.

I felt like I was hanging by the proverbial slender thread in the program. I was hoping against hope that the instructor pilot got enough satisfaction out of chewing my ass that he would not tell the captain in charge of this class about my transgression. When I was handed my grade slip I noticed the other students got A's and I got my one and only D with "failure to follow instructions" listed in writing on the checklist. Beyond that I hoped that it would not get back to the TAC officers in my section and was relieved that it did not result in a failing grade for the flight lesson. It did give me a wake-up call about listening, remembering details, and paying attention to following the directions of the instructors. I realized this was a high-risk environment where mistakes or lack of attention could have serious consequences. I know the instructor was right to stop me in my tracks and come down on me with a ton of bricks. I was thankful that he didn't take it to the next level and advocate a heave-ho higher up the chain of command. These instructors were mostly Vietnam veterans, and when they made a point, we listened.

Confined area training proved useful in the Delta when landing in some of the small hamlets, soccer fields in the middle of town squares, or very small openings in the jungle with heavy loads of supplies or people. The early training was a valued resource.

Fort Wolters, Texas
June 11, 1968

Dear Mom, Dad, and Family,

...I passed my advance standardization ride on Monday with a good score and wound up academics with about an 85% average on the final weather test. Weather is an accredited course and transfers 3 credits to any college.... I am finished with cross-country work and over the next 2 weeks I will deal with the fundamentals of formation flying.... I will leave for Fort Rucker on 23 July (1967) and I will forward my new address as soon as I learn what it is.... Dave White, the candidate I came home at Christmas with, has a new Ford and is driving down. He plans to stop in New Orleans and it would be very interesting to see that city....

Love
Your Son, Fred

*   *   *

Warrant Officer Candidate School was demanding, as was learning to fly a helicopter. As any pilot will tell you, your self-esteem gets all caught up and confused in flight training. Your personal identity gets wrapped up in whether you can make it through the military discipline on the one hand

and the rigors of trying to master a machine that seems to defy being controlled on the other. As candidates we were often locked in an "us versus them" relationship with our TAC officers and our flight instructors. Few of them seemed interested in our personal self-esteem. It was not uncommon to get yelled at or beat on the helmet by your flight instructor after not performing a maneuver to an instructor's standard. We all feared the shame and failure of being removed from the program.

I felt this in a personal way because, as I mentioned before, I looked young and inexperienced for my age, and I didn't get the military discipline part at first. My area in the barracks was destroyed day after day during inspection time by the TAC officers. This not only discouraged me but also angered my friends in the company who supported me and helped me learn to play the game of being organized in my personal effects in the Army way. We frequently commiserated once again about the three ways to look at life: the right way, the wrong way, and the Army way. In a desperate attempt to get me shaped up or shipped out, I was given command of the company by the tactical staff officers. However, the skill that saved my ass was my loud voice and enjoyment of making up verses for calling cadence while we were marching.

When anyone learns to fly a helicopter, the first couple of hours after the introduction, flying straight and level, turns, climbs and descents through the air, involves learning how to hover. This activity seems beyond comprehension, requires the coordinated use of all extremities at once, and for quite a while seems undoable. Then all of a sudden, after lots of practice and scaring the shit out of your instructor and yourself, it all starts to fit together for most students. It goes faster for some and takes a lot longer for others. A good friend, Mike, was struggling with this challenge, and once it starts to go sideways it can be a real bear to bring it back into your wheelhouse. Of course, the hatchet that is hanging over your head is that if you can't learn to hover, you can't stay in the program, so it is a high-stakes phase of the training. Mike was brought in and told he was being set back a class for more instruction and to master hovering. We all felt terrible for him. Mike was standing outside his barracks and looking a little down.

Here were the words to the "Jody" we called out as we went by in formation. His nickname was "Foxy." I had two nicknames during flight school: My first one was "Jingles" because I lost my voice at one point and sounded like Andy Devine, sidekick of Wild Bill Hickok in the Western television series. My second one was "Flyer Tuck" because of my seminarian background, and naturally quite often it got modified to something profane that sounded similar.

Foxy Foxy Don't be blue
You'll be right there with us too
Am I right or wrong? You're right!
Tell me if I'm wrong! You're right!
Sound off, one two, Sound off three four
Cadence count one, two three four,
one two, three four.

Graduating from the primary flight training program at Fort Wolters, Texas, was quite a milestone accomplishment for me. I had survived the rigors of discipline, harassment, and military flight instruction. I was halfway through my flight training program, and my scores and performance indicated I was doing well and learning to be an Army aviator. I had demonstrated my leadership ability to our TAC officers and I had learned to be better organized in both my personal gear and in approaching my classroom assignments. I was learning to turn criticism into personal acknowledgment of performance limitations and to push myself harder to succeed in each required academic area. I was aware of appropriate military bearing and proud to be pursuing being a warrant officer in the U.S. Army. I carried myself with more assurance and had learned how to inspire confidence in my peers. These were remarkable changes for me to achieve in a four-month time frame.

Graduation from the primary flight program at Fort Wolters was a very important activity for me. The seminary I had been enrolled in did not have a formal graduation from high school for a variety of reasons. We did not receive a paper high school diploma because the program was designed to include the first two years of college. At the flight school graduation many parents, wives, family and friends were in attendance. Our TAC officers were present, as were the commander of the fort and a number of his leadership team in the post theater. We received the silver wings of an Army aviator to place on our uniform after an impressive graduation ceremony. I had ordered a flight school ring that has been a treasured possession all my life. It was inscribed with my class number 67–19 and the words "Above the Best," the motto of Army Aviation. As the program finished, the band and a chorus played and sang the Army Aviation song. It was one of the proudest moments of my young life and one I still fondly remember.

"Winged Soldiers"—The Army Aviation Song

We're winged soldiers
(spoken) I am an American fighting man. An Army aviator serving with the forces that make our country free. I will never forget my duty, my men, my honor. I will trust in my God, my country, and my ship.
Winged soldiers are we....

Saber wings will lift us when we get the call
Through the dawn like eagles we will soar

Roll the pitch and throttle. Cyclic to the wall
Listen to the Army eagles roar

We're winged soldiers
We fly above the best
Defenders of the land and the free
From the sky we do or die
And let the angels rest Winged soldiers are we.

Charging through the jungle
Hear our rotors roar
Down from in the valley towards the hill
Fighting aviators out to win the war
Here comes the Army's escadrille

Rotor blades are turning
Diving towards the fire
Screaming in like eagles for the kill
After our inferno, troopers must admire Eagles of the Army's escadrille.

*   *   *

When we completed the primary phase of our flight training, we graduated at Fort Wolters, and our next duty assignment was Fort Rucker, Alabama. We had a few days allocated for us to make travel arrangements to get there. I went there in a private vehicle with other warrant officer candidates who shared expenses for the trip. Along the way we travelled through a number of Southern towns and spent a couple of days in New Orleans, Louisiana. There we were intrigued by the unique ambiance of that city. In particular we enjoyed the Cajun food, the exotic drinks, the Zydeco music, the quirky souvenir stores, and the notoriously bawdy behavior of the locals and tourists on Bourbon Street.

When we arrived at Fort Rucker, it looked a lot like Fort Polk, Louisiana. The World War II barracks and support service areas all looked like the familiar vestiges of an old Army fort. This was actually a comfortable feeling of beginning to feel a fit with military life. The differences were not at first readily discernible. The heliport, aircraft, outlying practice fields, and level of sophistication of the instrument and tactical instruction soon consumed the majority of our focus. It was quite a feeling to be entering a distinctly different second phase of our training. There was a perceptible air of seriousness about the purpose of each training session and a sense of getting very close to the whole reason we had been involved in all this training, to prepare us to be going into combat in the very near future.

We learned where the important facilities were located in relation to our assigned barracks. The PX, the movie theater, and various informal eating and relaxing areas were accounted for in the post. It was a place where you could feel safe and secure in your surroundings. We never needed to lock our possessions up in our barracks or be concerned about things getting stolen. There was a code about being in the warrant officer program that was very clear about honesty and respect.

Fort Rucker, Alabama
Thursday, July 27, 1967

Dear Mom, Dad, and Family,

…went to New Orleans for 2 days en route here. We saw the French Quarter…. I started taking instrument training in a Bell TH13 helicopter. We don't even see the ground for the next 50 hrs except for entering and leaving the traffic pattern at the heliport. They lost 2 students and IPs in a mid-air last class. Mid airs between helicopters are very rare but traumatic for the remaining students and instructor pilots. With so many helicopters in the air at one time doing training exercises, we all had our head on a swivel looking for other aircraft…. We wear a hood on our helmet and our vision is limited by panels to the instrument panel. This kind of flying requires constant effort, concentration and crosscheck between about 15 primary and secondary instruments and gauges. It can be very tiring and fatiguing. The temperature and humidity here are ridiculous. I long for a cool breeze off Puget Sound back home. We usually come out of the bubble after 2 hours soaked with hardly a dry thread on us. Our academic classes cover how the instruments work and radio navigation aids….

Love,
Your Son,
Fred

Our instrument training was done in a Bell TH13 helicopter. This helicopter is a popular two-seat helicopter with a clear bubble enclosure around the pilots and cockpit area and a tail cone that is open tubes and looks sort of like an Erector Set. It's the helicopter that you see in old *M*A*S*H* television shows. It is a very reliable helicopter and a more stable platform, and that is why it is used for teaching instrument flying. The sun in Alabama gets very hot this time of the year and it is over 100 degrees in the cockpit some afternoons. We wore a hood most of the time that limited our vision to the instrument panel, and it was one of the more challenging phases of our flight training. We would fly most of the lesson referencing the instruments to take off, climb, level off, follow a specific radial of an electronic beacon, practice holding patterns, descend, do unusual attitudes, approaches and even practice engine failures and autorotations with this vision restriction in place. My instructor for this phase was very forceful and he enjoyed really turning up the heat and making his students sweat. He was what we call "a helmet thumper" and didn't mince words or actions if we got disoriented or weren't exactly sure of our position in space. I struggled a bit with visualizing our position with respect to a specific radial of a particular instrument approach but ended up mastering the skills and getting passing grades in this phase. Each of the beacons was named for a place in Vietnam, like Bear Cat or Can Tho. Most pilots struggled to some degree to become proficient in this type of flying, but it is essential to master because studies have shown that if you fly a helicopter into a cloud bank and lose visual reference, after three to five minutes most pilots who don't have instrument flight training will become disoriented and lose control of the helicopter. We received a tactical instrument rating upon program completion that was designed to help you get out of inadvertently flying into the clouds and getting back out by making a 180-degree turn to return to an area of visual-flight-rules type weather.

Fort Rucker, Alabama
Tuesday, August 8, 1967

Dear Mom, Dad, and Family,

…I now have 14 hours of instrument flying. After staring at these instruments for an hour and half they seem to jump all over the cockpit. I still have so much to do in academics and in keeping my uniforms and room in proper order.

Next weekend we are learning physical combat, taking the Physical Training (PT) test. Then the following week we qualify with the 45 pistol and then the M-16 rifle sometime in the future. The courses are getting involved with complex radar approaches and civilian air traffic control procedures … picked up 2 books from a civilian instructor for the FAA commercial helicopter rating. We can take the written test on the day we graduate. It consists of 50 questions, no flight test required, and if I pass I get a civilian FAA rating as a commercial helicopter pilot. It is the equivalent of $10,000 of flight time in a civilian helicopter.

We are getting close to why we're learning all of this and all the goofing around is pretty well out of the picture. Even the short weekend from noon Saturday to Sunday might usually find me getting display articles, doing laundry, or hitting the books. I guess it doesn't sound much like me. But we have to just about live this aviation experience because whatever we learn may save our rear-ends in the very near future.

Love
Your Son,
Fred

Fort Rucker, Alabama
Wednesday, September 20, 1967

Dear Mom, Dad, and Family,

Well I passed my advanced instrument check ride … next Monday we will go into the tactics phase and begin the transition into the turbine powered Hueys … classes are now dealing with the functioning and breakdown of the standard turbine engines used in the aircraft we will be flying. It's more or less of a basic knowledge because it would take too long to run us through the standard mechanic's course. The purpose is so that we can recognize and relate possible engine troubles in certain terms for quick repair adjustment or whatever. There will be a crew chief in every ship responsible for keeping it in the air. But they want us to know what's happening too.

…still the thick humid Southern air that seems to gag you every time you come out of an air-conditioned classroom. I flew fixed wing last weekend for about three hours. Mostly just doing landings and takeoffs and generally just staying in the traffic pattern trying different techniques in crosswinds and getting proficient. This coming Saturday we will begin various air maneuvers working towards the commercial fixed wing pilot's license.

I become a senior on Monday. This privilege will last until we graduate. It's the last rank step in the candidate program and the final 2-month period before becoming an officer.

Love,
Your Son, Fred

*   *   *

Few words conjure up a vision that no pilot wants to think about, but some do. A midair collision occurred during instrument training in the class before me that cost the lives of two instructors and two students. When helicopters run into each other in the air the results are almost always catastrophic in terms of loss of life and aircraft. A helicopter is a marvel of aviation technology. It is a finely balanced gyroscope that flies. It includes weight-balanced mechanical equipment, fuel, oil, fluids, and personnel and an engine that powers spinning components, the rotor system and the tail rotor. Controls are manipulated by the pilot to move it forward, backward, sideways, up and down. When everything functions as designed the helicopter can be an extension of the pilot and help the pilot accomplish both life-saving and life-taking missions.

In flight school during the Vietnam War buildup there were routinely hundreds of training helicopters in the air at one time. The program of instruction was articulated down to the finest detail. Traffic patterns were laid out around Army training heliports and between outlying practice fields and the heliport. "Roads in the sky" were literally created with the use of large markers at visual checkpoints on the ground with specified altitudes, airspeeds, and traffic separation to be adhered to when crossing each marker. The student pilot and instructor practiced regular and required visual scans and communications prior to turns, climbs, and descents, or emergency procedures. In spite of all of these precautions, there was the opportunity for pilot error with devastating results. It was always unsettling when one of these events occurred whether in training or in combat. I am reminded of the cautionary maxim that every pilot has in mind when flying: Flying like the sea is not inherently dangerous. It is, however, very unforgiving of the least bit of inattention or operator error.

Fort Rucker, Alabama
Sunday, October 8, 1967

Dear Mom, Dad, and Family,

It's Sunday morning and I've been restricted to the Company area. I neglected to dust my lamp for 3 days in a row and I went before the Major for flagrant neglect of my personal gear. He read me Article 31 and threatened me with an Article 15…. It's been a long nine months of getting nothing but harassment, restriction, and ridden in general but two more months isn't very long and I'll make it.

Yesterday morning we had an artillery demonstration…. Four students went up in each Huey and each took a turn calling fire missions in on some targets about 2 miles away. The firing battery consisted of six howitzers and a firing adjustment team. We were all impressed with the amount of firepower that was put out by the big guns and noted the effect of different types of charges on the target. It was a very interesting and informative morning.

In flying I am working on pinnacles, confined areas, ridgelines, and standard maneuvers at the stage field. In instrument flying we are learning how to operate the radios in the Huey….

> Love,
> Your Son,
> Fred

> Fort Rucker, Alabama
> Saturday, October 15, 1967

Dear Mom, Dad, and Family,

…I guess that fall is here at last. We all welcome the cooler weather though it sometimes presents some problems to flying. Two nights ago we were ferrying aircraft back to the heliport from one of the outlying tactical fields about 30 mi away. The weather moved down fast and thick fog enshrouded the control zone. The pilot in command went on instruments and I kept a watch out for the landing lights. Lightening flashed about us and a steady rain brought the visibility down to almost O/O … all 25 of the ships made it without incident and the flight commander commended us on our ability and keeping our cool in the adverse conditions. It was an experience that we all benefitted from in confidence and appreciation for those 50 grueling hours of instrument training.

During the last week we have been performing various assigned missions. Reconnaissance of routes, landing zones, navigation, operating with internal loads and external sling loads…. Position reports must be given precisely on time and at the proper control points. We also were familiarized with formation flying at night and will get more of that next week.

Next weekend we have escape and evasion training. Then the following two weeks we spend most of the time in the field on twenty-four-hour alert simulating Viet Nam situations.

> Love,
> Your Son,
> Fred

On the weekends, I began taking more fixed-wing lessons at a small airfield on the outskirts of Fort Rucker in Ozark, Alabama. I had an excellent instructor. He enjoyed flying and teaching me how to control the little Cessna 150 airplane. He had been a corporate pilot and was now working for the Army instructing helicopter pilots at Fort Rucker, and he enjoyed keeping his certified flight instructor ratings for airplanes current as well.

The field was a very down-home flight operation, with an asphalt runway that had a few potholes in it and a mom-and-pop type of flight operation where they knew your name and seemed interested in your flight progress. It proved to be great for learning rough field takeoffs and crosswind landings.

We had more freedom in our schedules as we got further into our flight training, especially on the weekends. When others headed to the beach in Panama City, Florida, or went on family outings if they were married and their wives had come to visit, I would find a way to get out to the local airport and enjoyed taking fixed-wing flying lessons.

Students were inevitably short of money and I could always find someone willing to lend their old car or motorcycle for a tank full of gas.

I knew by this time that a warrant officer, after graduation, could take a written examination and get a commercial helicopter license from the FAA. I also wanted to get a commercial fixed-wing rating, and that could be done as well with a written and flight test and it became my goal to obtain these licenses before I went to Vietnam. I was thinking down the road of possibly being an airline pilot, if I made it out of Vietnam. When I was home on leave prior to leaving for Vietnam, I took a checkride in the Seattle area at the Renton Airport and was awarded a commercial fixed-wing crossover license. Flying was really in my blood, and even on leave home I found time to take a tour offered by the FAA of the Air Route Traffic Control Center just outside of Seattle.

Fort Rucker, Alabama
Friday, October 20, 1967

Dear Mom and Dad

...as my stick-buddy and I were running up the Huey for a pre–take off check, the fire detection warning light came on and you never saw two people shut down a turbine engine and bail out of that cockpit any faster. It all turned out to be a short in the wiring but it was an experience to say the least.

I am going out for our tactics briefing this afternoon. The call sign of our flight is "Knight" and looks like a pretty good bunch. We will have 15 hours solo and 10 hours dual in this final phase. We will be doing route recons, airmobile assaults, medevacs and similar missions.

I'm looking forward to seeing everyone sometime around Thanksgiving if all goes well. Current academics deal with tactical principles and the relationship of various branches in a division. We have to have a fairly good understanding of the relationship of various units as we will oftentimes be in direct support of the infantry or artillery etc. We are all a little apprehensive about our assignments but we have been hearing nothing else for 9 months so we are anxious to find out what the story really is.

Love,
Your Son
Fred

Fort Rucker, Alabama
Friday, October 27, 1967

Dear Mom, Dad, and Family,

This week we had classes on how, when, and where to drop aircraft flares for the best and most effective illumination, computing for winds etc. Another day dealt with new and old radios and navigation aids for direction finding and voice communications. And today we started a 10-hour block on the adjustment of artillery fire from aircraft. This is an important role of Army Aviation in Vietnam and is quite involved with geometric angles, requesting radio procedures, and the adjustment of fire upon the enemy, the type of fire desired for the mission to be accomplished.

Tomorrow will get in another fixed wing lesson in the afternoon. In the morning we have an inspection in greens and a few lectures on the protocol of being an officer etc. I should be taking my advanced instrument check ride next week and hoping to do well. Orders came down for the class 2 ahead of us. 3 went to school for a tandem rotor helicopter (Chinook), 6 got stateside assignments, and all of the rest went to Vietnam aviation units....

Love,
Your Son,
Fred

Fort Rucker, Alabama
Sunday, November 5, 1967

Dear Mom, Dad, and Family,

...in the advanced instrument phase of training. Instructors are military recent veterans of Vietnam, think they own the world and treat us like dirt. Not very enjoyable. The days are very long and everyone counts the days when the phase will be over and quite reluctantly looks forward to the next flying period. Have taken up my fixed wing lessons and should have my commercial fixed wing rating when I graduate from the school. My instructor for that is a real nice guy who taught basic instruments and moonlights instructing fixed wing time on the side. He used to fly a commercial twin engine for a corporation in upper New York. He has over 9,000 hours in various aircraft.... Next week I qualify with M-16 and hear the 1st in a series of overseas lectures. I got a 92 on my basic instrument check ride—one of the highest in the class but having a real tough time in advanced. Two weeks ago went through the gas chamber and qualified with a 45 caliber pistol also took physical PT test and did fairly well.

Love,
Your Son
Fred

Seattle, WA
December 1, 1967—

Dear Mom, Dad, and Family,

I guess I have never been one for sentimental good-byes so I decided I would write this letter. I think during this leave we came the closest to getting together, especially so on Thanksgiving, when we sang and got along so well. You were most understanding and especially so in regards to use of the car. I look forward sincerely to Vietnam, naturally with a bit of apprehension, but more for the wider perspective it will give me on life, and how I can best use my talents in this world.

Dad, I am taking your Legion of Merit medal with me. Nana left it with me at the time of our short visit. I don't think I will ever be half the soldier you were just by the nature of my personality, nevertheless, I will do my best as I did in flight school I will write often and relate what I can from my experiences

I don't have a will. I think it is unnecessary in our family, but should a situation arise, I would like to see a portion of the money go to Fircrest School or some such cause after the majority of it goes to the family. I realize the chance is remote but just in case.

Well to wind it up, please keep this letter within the house and just between you, mom and dad. I think it would be best that way. I will appreciate your prayers. You will all be in mine as poor and as infrequent at times that they may be. Take care. I love you all very much and will see you in about a year, God willing,

Love,
Your Son
Fred

5

Welcome to Vietnam!

After the long flight from the United States that stopped for fuel in Guam and then proceeded to Vietnam, I remember the tension level in the cabin rising as they announced we were beginning our descent into Tan Son Nhut Airport at Saigon. We were letting down into a war zone. Some of us wouldn't be coming home from this adventure. Would the plane be shot at as we descended? What part of Vietnam would we be assigned to? What would Saigon be like? Would we get to spend any time there before being sent out to our unit? Where would we be assigned and how dangerous would the assignment be?

As the plane got lower on approach, the vegetation and military hardware looked strange and foreboding. We held our breath as we turned final and lined up to touch down on the runway. Then we were down, and the humidity of the air hit us as the doors were opened and we deplaned down the stairway. After a briefing for a general welcome, we were divided into groups of officers and enlisted men. We rode in a bus that had chain link fencing on the windows. This, we were told, was to prevent grenades from being thrown in the windows at us. After dropping our green canvas gear bags in the assigned barracks we had some time to wander around Saigon. It was a busy city of motorbikes, strange sounds and smells, and lots of attractive young women dressed in colorful áo dàis standing in the doorways of various restaurants and bars along the streets of the city. There was no question about their intentions as they invited us to come into their bar or restaurant.

Saigon was an interesting mix of sights, sounds, and aromas of the Orient. It was a city of stark contrasts consisting of impressive French colonial architecture and churches and yet was also well known for gambling dens, prostitution, and opium. There were businessmen walking down the streets in shirts and ties and children playing in the streets who were barefoot and dressed in rags. Popular American music emanated from the bars along the main streets. GIs rode in rickshaws pedaled by young men, and women carried baskets of fruit and vegetables on their heads. The population was 1.5 million in the "Paris of the East." It seemed like the preferred

Saigon, the Paris of the East. A feast filled with forbidden pleasures and intrigue. Wall-to-wall people hurrying to their appointments. Scooters and rickshaws competing with each other for room on the roadway. The smells of garbage and strange aromas of food cooking. Beautiful young women in the doorways of restaurants and bars beckoning passersby to enter their world. Music and laughter and fun awaits. Opium dens and prostitution. Marijuana and hashish. The base flight surgeon's warnings about who you are with and what might happen to you if you make the wrong choices. Stately cathedrals, Buddhist monasteries, municipal buildings and people intent on making the next streetlight. School-aged children in their uniforms with book bags and lunches walking in groups towards their schools. People lying in the gutter and the overwhelming stew of human, animal, vegetable, insect, etc., assaulting your senses. Coffee and beignets, strange menu choices, flashbacks of reading *The Orient Express*, *The African Queen*. Where will I be going tomorrow in my first assignment? Will I ever get out of this place alive? Isn't this exciting and the adventure you were looking for? Or is it?

form of transportation was a bike or motor scooter. We had drinks and dinner and enjoyed exchanging pleasantries with the bar girls, but we stopped short of the offers for "a real good time." We returned to our dorm-style transition bunk area and retired for our first night's sleep in Vietnam.

That night something crawled across my face while I slept and I reached up to grab a cockroach the size of my thumb. This wakeup call convinced me that we weren't in Kansas anymore. This was the real deal. We were in Saigon, and tomorrow we would be leaving the big city for our own assignments in the combat zone.

After our night in the barracks at Long Binh, we were briefed about the four Corps Areas (I, II, III, IV) of South Vietnam and some basic information about the combat situation and then we were told our assignments. I was assigned to the 121st Assault Helicopter Company in the IV Corps area in the Mekong Delta near a town called Soc Trang, about 100 miles south of Saigon.

Helicopters arrived shortly afterward. One of them had a tiger head with a lightning bolt painted on the cockpit doors, and we loaded up our duffel bags and strapped in the back seats for our first in-country ride to our newly assigned base. The aircraft lifted off from the helipad and climbed up and departed south out of the traffic pattern. It was quite a sight to see Saigon from altitude. I remember seeing temples and rivers leading out to the South China Sea, palm trees, and roads filled with people and all manner of vehicles including motor scooters, bicycles, rickshaws, and trucks, travelling Highway 1 in and out of Saigon. When we got outside of the Long Binh area and in the country, the scenery changed from urban to rural and most of the country was wide-open rice paddies as far as we could see.

The Huey blades popped in their iconic syncopated rhythm and then the nose lowered, the popping got louder, and we started descending at about 100 knots. Before we knew it, we were down on the deck, at about treetop level, following the highway and flying from side to side in wide S turns and steeper banked turns for the next 90 miles of the trip. At one point the door gunners on either side fired their weapons into the open and unoccupied rice paddies below. When we came to a town, village, or temple we would rise a few feet higher and take a look at the surprised faces of people looking up at us from the pastoral scenes below. We crossed canals, bridges, small towns and farms and varied our altitude from five feet off the rice paddies to about 25 feet in the air. The scenery we observed included quite a few Buddhist temples that colorfully stood out in the small towns against the greenery of the surrounding rice paddies and nipa palm trees. The countryside was very flat, and each rice paddy was bounded by irrigation ditches and fed by neighboring canals and punctuated by larger rivers brown with sediment. To our left we could see the sea off in the distance, and to our right were the faint outlines of the mountains of South Vietnam. This ride was for the amusement of the crew and to welcome us to the Mekong Delta IV Corps area of Vietnam. It was definitely an exciting way to get to our assigned base. Later, these low-level welcomes were discontinued when fire was taken and a passenger was shot and killed on one of these runs. There was a war going on, and adding joyrides to the welcome trip became a thing of the past in our company.

Night

It's night. The thick humid air hangs heavy in the sticky room.

I lie awake sweating.

Looking at the stark stucco walls and the shadow of a lizard darting across the ceiling.
The sounds are strange, oriental mixed with the clamor of modern machinery.
I think of a close call today. Of tomorrow

Of how I wish there was a woman here to soothe away the tensions and share the
tenderness of her touch with me.
An outgoing mortar round goes off and I start

More by instinct than desire, and then settle back knowing sleep will not come easily
    tonight.
Tomorrow I will wake and begin a new day Anxious to meet its new challenges
But tonight, tonight I ask myself "what in the hell am I doing here?"

> Soc Trang, Republic of Vietnam
> December 25, 1967

Mom, Dad, & Family, Merry Christmas.

I am with the 121st Assault Helicopter Company at Soc Trang in the heart of the
Delta. I had my in country check ride yesterday and will work for about 4 days on supply missions & milk runs before being ready to go on combat assaults.

The season is dry, the climate is very hot and humid. Our Company has very good
facilities, I have my own room in a tin roofed cement floor building. The airfield here is
relatively secure and well-guarded.

Vietnamese women do our laundry, shine our shoes, and clean our rooms for about
$10 a month. Poverty among the Vietnamese is almost too all-encompassing for words
but our money merely induces inflation and aggravates the problem.

…Flying in the Delta is relatively safe especially from the standpoint of engine failure as there are many fields in which to land, and much of the flying is in formation
so there is usually someone to pick you up. The company was short-handed and very
much overworked and was very glad to welcome us. They are a very close-knit group
and as usual we will have to prove ourselves to merit acceptance. I am very fortunate in
my assignment and glad to get off my fanny and into the air again.

> Love,
> Your Son, Fred

2000 Feet Below

A man died 2000 feet below
He went where he was told not to go At least he was supposed to know
He could have been rowing without a care

Not knowing he wasn't supposed to be there

But he was And so
2000 feet below

A man died and nobody cried I wonder why?

Soc Trang, Republic of Vietnam
Wednesday, January 3, 1968

Dear Dad,

… we are flying very long hours and I never seem to catch the post office when it's open.

There is lots of action occurring. They mortared us again two nights ago but there were no serious injuries. We are going on daily combat assaults lifting ARVN regulars in reactionary moves against a recent rise in Vietcong activity in the Delta. I have about 60 hours now of in country flight time and I am learning the ropes well. I'm actually getting a charge out of this and look forward to each day.

Love,
Your Son, Fred

Soc Trang, Vietnam
Tuesday, January 9, 1968

Dear Mom, Dad, and Family,

I had an interesting mission last night. We flew "firefly." We have an aircraft mounted with 7 searchlights in a cluster and a 50 caliber machine gun. With two gunships as escort we go up and down the canals & roads at night looking for enemy activity after curfew hours. We got a few tracers fired at us but no significant action. We flew from 8pm at night until 6am in the morning … all night long. I slept in this morning and as I see the mission board I am up for a combat assault early tomorrow morning so I must get to bed. I got your first letter. It was real interesting. Please keep them coming. Everything is fine and time is passing quickly. I am very interested in this type of flying and couldn't get this experience anywhere else.

Love,
Your Son, Fred

*   *   *

Sometimes our assigned mission involved flying out to Navy ships off the coast or in the rivers of the Delta. In many cases, this involved landing on a small helipad where through the chin bubble you saw only water. The crew chief talked the pilot down onto the pad on approach, keeping the tail rotor and main rotor clear of antennas, etc. on the ship. Takeoffs were exciting as well, especially if the helicopter had a full load of fuel and people or supplies. The aircraft would be lifted to a hover and then nose over to obtain translational lift and often settled somewhat towards the water before transitioning to forward flight. This maneuver evoked a feeling we called "pucker factor" in the pilots as we held our breath hoping that translational lift would occur before we dumped the whole aircraft in the drink. It was worth it, though, since the Navy always seemed to eat better than we did and it was a special treat to have a steak or ice cream at a meal on board ship.

I also had the opportunity to support the Mobile Riverine Force and Navy PBRs (Patrol Boat Riverine) and PCFs (Patrol Craft Fast) Swift Boats

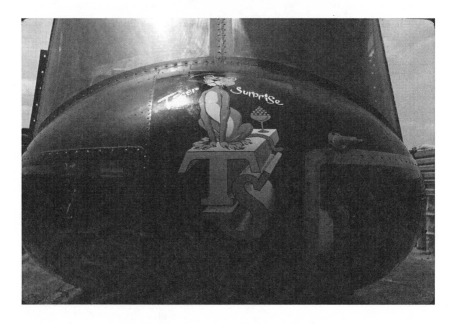

During my tour as a Tiger I was able to fly a number of missions in a transport helicopter that was called *Viking Surprise*. It was a regular slick transport
helicopter equipped with a high-intensity cluster of landing lights in the cargo
area, M60 machine guns, and at one point a 50-caliber machine gun. This was
an exciting assignment, and I flew on these missions as a Tiger with two aircraft commanders, Frank Orifici and Hal Duensing. We would cruise the canals
around the area looking for enemy sampan traffic at night and, if we found
them, turn on the light and engage them. If they fired back at us or turned out
to be in sampans laden with weapons or explosives, we would call the gunships
on airfield standby for some heavy-duty rockets, grenades, or machine gun fire.
This helicopter later became *Tiger Surprise.* In May of 1970 the aircraft was hit
with an enemy B-40 rocket and destroyed.

(when their own team of gunships, the Seawolves, was down for maintenance and the Vikings were called to assist). I was impressed that they
would venture up the little canals in a small PBR with a machine gun
mounted on the bow. It seems like they frequently stirred up a rat's nest and
had little room to turn around or retreat. The crews of the aluminum hulled
Swift Boats were equally courageous. One of the most impressive weapons
used for clearing out areas along the larger rivers was called Zippo. Like its
name implied, it released a stream of flame that scorched the earth for what
looked from above like a football field to remove places for snipers to hide
along the riverbanks and among the mangrove jungle trees and to discour-
age them from engaging passing Navy boats or the sampans of local farmers on the way to market.

Soc Trang, Vietnam
Wednesday, January 10, 1968

Dear Nana,

...it's 9:00pm. I've been flying since 5:30am taking ARVN troops in on combat assaults. The night before last I flew the "light ship" with searchlights mounted on it in a cluster. We patrol the canals and roads for curfew violators from 8:00pm to 6AM in the morning. When we find them they are dealt with by a 50-caliber machine gun mounted in the cargo compartment. We drew a few tracers shot at us but no real action.

Our field was only mortared once last week Charlie must be taking a rest. Don't worry Nana. I really enjoy this flying and wouldn't have it anyway else. I'm just glad I'm not stuck at a desk somewhere. I will keep you posted through mom.

Love,
Your Grandson,
Fred

*   *   *

Each unit in Vietnam had its own level of expectations, uniform rules, operating procedures, and military bearing requirements, etc. Sometimes these changed quite a bit with the change of commanders. Our unit was very mission-oriented with commonly held expectations for flight operations, but there were areas where we were given quite a bit of latitude to express personal identity and preferences. A couple of them were how we decorated our living areas and the personal weapons we acquired from others during our tour. Stereo equipment was becoming very popular for listening to the music of the 1960s, and one of the first purchases each new pilot or flight crewmember tried to make included an amplifier/tuner with a name like Panasonic; a turntable for records, two large speakers in wooden cases, maybe called Akai or Sansui; and a Teac tape deck for recording everything from the latest records to the latest mortar attack sounds.

Our aircraft had personalized logos that were usually either on the nose cone or front side doors of each helicopter and specific to that tail number. At the beginning of my tour, we were allowed to paint our flight helmets with various symbols and graphics. These artistic expressions ran the gamut from unit logos to cartoon characters, obscene expressions and gestures, to Playboy bunnies, from the sublime to the ridiculous, based on aviation history, the creative ideas of the crew chiefs and pilots of our unit, and the tolerance level of the commanding officer. Many of the examples of iconic ones from the Vietnam War feature designs from my own unit, the 121st Assault Helicopter Company. This artwork often brought a smile to the people we flew supplies in to or sometimes gave a sense of ownership and pride to the crew maintaining the aircraft. It seemed to lighten the load and brighten everyone's day a little to be working on an aircraft named

Captain Klutz was a cartoon character created by artist Don Martin in 1967, a parody of all of the superhero comic strip characters of the time. He was forever falling all over himself making mistakes. He was featured in some editions of *Mad* magazine and was popular among young people in the 1960s. The artists in downtown Soc Trang were very good at replicating these figures, and we weren't worried about appropriating them for use on our helicopters. What were they going to do, send us back to Vietnam for copyright infringement? I'm sure Captain Klutz brought a smile to many faces when he landed to resupply some outpost in the Delta.

Harvey with an old, grizzled pilot's face on the nose or "What, Me Worry?" and a picture of Alfred E. Newman out front.

I was a Blue Tiger for the first five months of my tour, and so I took my helmet into a local painter in a shop in Soc Trang and had him paint it metallic blue with our yellow and black Tiger logo on the back that included a lightning bolt and a red Maltese cross on each side of the helmet.

There was one Tiger helicopter named after the movie *The Pink Panther*, and so the aircraft commander had his helmet painted pink to match the aircraft logo. On a combat assault he took a round above his head in the aircraft and had second thoughts about how much the pink helmet stood out as a target compared to the olive drab color of our helicopters. Coincidentally, the introduction of a ballistic olive drab colored replacement/upgrade helmet occurred system-wide shortly after the painted helmet phase. By that time, Tet of 1968 had happened and we were more than happy to present a lower profile to the Viet Cong after getting shot at so much. The painted helmet phase sort of ran its course over time, and ultimately the pilots in our unit wore the new olive drab ballistic helmets that supposedly offered us more protection.

During my tour we were first issued a .45 caliber pistol and a brown leather shoulder harness to wear it across the chest. I went downtown to Soc Trang and bought a black Western cowboy-type holster with loops all around the belt for about 20 .45 caliber bullets. The .45 is a powerful pistol, and the rounds are hefty and I'm told will stop a person. I slept with mine loaded and under my pillow with my clothes on and my pants down around my ankles when I was first in-country and we were getting mortared somewhat frequently. I guess I'm lucky I didn't have a bad dream and shoot myself in the night. Halfway through my tour they collected the .45s and issued us a .38 Police Special. I thought it felt a little lightweight, but it was considered an improvement by somebody at a higher pay grade than me.

Some of the nose art on our helicopters was whimsical and cartoon-like. Other artwork bordered on the obscene. Some evoked the camaraderie of the company. This one was a mixture of comic art and a reminder that the aircraft and the armed soldiers that were on her were capable of devouring the enemy. There is a fear that is instilled in the enemy when the word "cannibal" is mentioned. I'm sure that the creators of this nose art had both messages in mind. Sometimes, after particularly difficult missions when there was downtime after refueling and maintaining the aircraft, self-designated artists would paint threatening messages on the underside of the helicopter or on the rockets we were sending their way.

Soc Trang, Vietnam
Tuesday, January 23, 1968

Dear Mom, Dad, and Family,

... involved in resupply missions, combat assaults, and various courier runs. They all make up an average week. On my down days I am working on a yearbook for the company that has to be ready by March....

A few days ago a friend of mine and I came across a couple of guitars that the special services people had in their center. We had a good time running through many old folksongs. There really isn't enough time to start a group here because all of our down days are staggered for scheduling purposes and depend on aircraft availability. [This man was Warrant Officer Ricky Lee Hull. He died during Tet a couple of weeks after this letter was written. The circumstances around the accident were very confusing. Their slick went down on a supply mission not far from Soc Trang and all four crewmembers died. It looked like they might have been shot down and a post-crash fire ensued.]

I have 150 hrs of flight time in now. I am going into town this morning to find a bedspread and maybe some curtains for my room, and just plain poke around a few of the small shops.

The Vietnamese New Year called "Tet" is coming in about 10 days. Lasts 8 days they go wild with firecrackers, weapons and firewater and its best to avoid going to town then, so am going now to pick up a few things. Everything here in the Delta is fine. The weather is comfortably warm and the rice fields are burning as the harvest season is ending. I will write again soon and am doing well.

Love,
Your Son, Fred

*   *   *

Getting a haircut on our airfield was not your ordinary experience. The local Vietnamese gentleman had a professional-looking shop and barber chair in the middle of our compound over by the chapel and the water supply/swimming pool. When I went in there, I was the only one in the shop. The barber would greet you with a bow and ask you how you would like your hair cut. You were given a shave with about a 12-inch-long straight razor that was sharpened in your presence on a long leather strap.

I often thought it felt strangely foreboding that he had that straight razor so close to my neck. It turned out later in my tour that it was determined that someone had given the local Viet Cong a map of our base during Tet that included where the officers and flight crewmembers were billeted. I heard that it was suspected that this individual had been the source of that information. Even now, in my golden years, I can feel the cold steel of that straight razor against my neck when I think of the many times I trustingly sat in his chair. As he finished cutting your hair and giving you a shave, he would apply some aromatic aftershave to the finished product. Every procedure he conducted was done with style and grace as if you were preparing to go out for an evening on the town. Some of us referred to the whole experience as getting a haircut from the Barber of Seville.

The haircut ended with him giving you the finishing touches of pulling on each of your fingers and both of your arms and cracking your neck in a couple of directions. Then he would finish you off by running an electronic palm hand massager over your shoulders, arms, and head. By then you were on the verge of falling asleep in his chair and it would be time to get up and pay the man for his time and effort. All in all, it was a pleasant, relaxing experience and a welcome respite from daily life on the airfield.

> Soc Trang, Vietnam
> Saturday, January 27, 1968

Dear Nana,

We just got through watching "combat" on the movie screen. It's the most popular film here. Everyone goes to see how it really is.... I sleep at night without fear of bombing but they mortar us anyway. (I remember sleeping in my uniform with my boots on and a 45 pistol under my pillow ready to run to the bunker by the Tiger's Den when the siren on the tower went off signaling incoming). It helps keep the arteries from hardening. Sometimes it's hard to tell if we are doing a lot of good. I think that the most important victories are in the attitudes of the people towards wanting to fight for freedom and that's a very hard thing to measure. I am enjoying the flying and time is passing quickly. I don't need anything.
Write when time allows.

> Love,
> Your Grandson,
> Fred

To Market

Down the canal in a sampan boat To the market place
With a load of rice
To haggle with friends about the price.

Pull, pull, pull to the steady driving beat.
Water slapping on the bow Spraying back on bare brown feet
Wondering who we're going to meet
And steering around the bend

But from the foliage on the shore A gun's retort, a bullet's bore
And the water is running red with fear The nearby boats all disappear

The word spreads rapidly all around Of a new location the VC have
     found And the fear remains for a day or so Till another rice farmer
     decides to go To market with a load of rice
To haggle with friends about the price.

> Soc Trang, Vietnam
> Saturday, January 27,1968

Mom, Dad, & Family,

...I was fortunate to draw a courier mission to a Navy LST (smaller type Navy vessel) anchored about 20 miles off the coast. I had a good lunch for a change with the officers on board. You couldn't give me their job on that boat for a year. They look bored to death. They patrol the waters for gun smuggling etc. Anyway I will say one thing, they eat a lot better than we do, but that's no top secret is it dad? Just the Army way. They said they wouldn't take our job for a fortune landing on that rolling boat…. I guess different things appeal to various people.

I flew the light ship one night and we ended up shooting up a couple of snipers who are among a VC Battalion who camp outside our airfield and keep the pilots on their toes with a little sporadic fire every now and then. The gunships have been shooting up the area pretty regularly so at least he knows that we are keeping tabs on him. The week went fast, many long hours flying, but it helped to pass the time.

Love,
Your Son,
Fred

Vietnamese Kids

Whenever we set the chopper down
A million kids gather around

These children are a little older. They liked to demonstrate their ability to speak English and engage you in conversation. Some brought things to sell and others just wanted to tell jokes or say something funny that would begin a conversation. Others were looking for money or food. We usually greeted them and had some opening exchange with them but made it very clear they were to stand back from the helicopter and not touch things. Some of the enemy soldiers we had encountered weren't too much older than some of them and of course there were stories of Americans being too trusting and finding themselves on the receiving end of losing their valuables or money.

Poking in here and looking in there
And generally getting in our hair.
And they laugh and say "OK, OK."
And salute us in the American Way
And they horse around as little kids do
They get out of hand
And we make them skidoo

And they come right back to get in our hair
Like little kids do everywhere
I think they're cool

6

Ash, Trash, and General
Little Minh

I was a new pilot to the unit, flying slicks with the Tigers, when we were assigned a single ship mission to resupply a Special Forces outpost in the Seven Mountains area along the Cambodian border. This beautiful area was characterized by wide stretches of green cropland, rice paddies, geometrically separated land areas, and steep mountains that jutted up from the valley floor. The outposts here were manned by Cambodians and supervised by Green Beret Special Forces personnel. It was stormy and raining, which added another couple of elements to the mix of the mission.

In the Seven Mountains area, there were concentrations of enemy hiding in caves on the mountainsides, usually well protected from hostile fire because of the steep and rugged terrain. They usually retreated into caves in the side of the mountains. We generally avoided flying near the mountain areas but stayed low over the valleys on resupply missions. We were navigating along the valley floor into and out of the outposts. The mission required shuttling cargo in and out of an outpost and avoiding rain showers that got quite heavy and disorienting at times. We were pushing the limits on fuel and were quite far away from a refueling station. As we navigated around the storm cells on one later run, we got a little disoriented and disagreed as a team where the location of the outpost had been.

Frank later disclosed that this had been one of his first missions as an aircraft commander and I was the co-pilot. We had been suspicious of the fuel gauges on this bird. They had been giving us some erroneous readings. As we searched for the outpost, the 20-minute low fuel light came on a bright yellow. After some back-and-forth with the tactical maps and banter about the disorienting weather, we finally located the outpost.

Frank made a pilot-in-command decision to call our base and ask that a drum of fuel be brought out by a maintenance ship to give us the fuel necessary to get home. The operations officer, who we all had some issues with at times anyway, decided to fly the mission of bringing us out the fuel. He didn't mince words with Frank about our fuel management and his need to bring it out to us. The fuel had to be pumped by hand into the tank. We returned safely to our base but our tale of having the fuel brought out to us was the subject of lots of ribbing that night in the Tigers' Den.

Frank was a good aircraft commander and a character as well. One time he had been flying all night long on airfield security, in a specially equipped transport helicopter we called Viking Surprise. This aircraft was a D model Huey that was equipped with a large spotlight, flares, and machine guns and was used to patrol the canals around Soc Trang at night. The mission was to search for Viet Cong moving enemy supplies, ammunition, and sometimes relocating their mortar tubes under the cover of darkness. When the crew of Surprise located the enemy, they would engage them with machine gun fire, and if there were multiple targets, they might alert a gunship team to come and assist them. The pilots who flew Viking Surprise were usually either Blue Tigers or White Tigers because it was a modified D model slick (transport-type) helicopter rather than a B model gunship.

As Frank attempted to get some rest the next day after being up all night, there were some Vietnamese workers who were mowing the lawn outside his hooch and they were taking a break and lying down on the sandbags stacked outside his window. The sandbags were there to protect the hooch and residents in the event of a mortar attack. They also provided a convenient place for workers to take a siesta away from the hot sun.

Frank opened the shutters and told them to "Di Di Mau" or "get out of here." The lawn workers seemed unmoved by his order, so to emphasize his request he emptied a fragmentation grenade, broke off the fuse, pulled the pin in the disabled grenade, opened the shutters again, and placed the grenade on the chest of the closest workman and shut the shutters. Needless to say, this sparked an immediate response from all of the workers, who dove in all directions. At the same time as this was occurring, our commanding officer, Major McNair, was coming out of his hooch in his Fruit of the Loom. He saw the grenade and hit the deck thinking it was a live grenade.

After a few minutes with no explosion the workers and Major McNair looked around at each other and determined that the grenade was not going to blow up, and so they returned to their previous activities a little unnerved by the experience. The workers dispersed and began mowing the lawn again, and Major McNair returned to his hooch.

When the dust settled, Frank was summoned to the commander's office where he was interrogated about the what and why of his actions. After listening to his report of the unfolding events, the commanding officer was not impressed with his actions and threatened him with an Article 15 for scaring the hell out of the workers and in particular for upsetting the company commander. Oddly enough, no further discipline was meted out.

Days passed with no further action, and Frank concluded that the incident had been forgotten and he would neither be dealing with a military discipline procedure nor face further consequences.

However, when a request came down for pilots from the 1st Cavalry up North, because they were in need of Loach pilots, Frank was one of the first transferred. He finished his tour flying these Light Observation Helicopters in hunter/killer teams paired up with a couple of Cobra gunships. It was a very high-risk assignment. The Cav. was known for its austere living arrangements (tents mostly) and for its aggressive approach to mission accomplishment.

> Soc Trang, Vietnam
> Thursday, February 8, 1968

Dear Mom, Dad, and Family,

It's 6 am in the morning. We have been on 24 hr alert since all this disturbance started. We are flying long days and sleeping in the helicopters at night. We are still getting mortared off and on but last night was quiet so maybe a new trend is starting. In the last 30 day period I have more hours of flight time than most pilots so I was given today off to go to bed. I had one day off about a week ago…. Mail is way behind because of all the fighting etc throughout Vietnam so I am anxious to get my hand in the mail bag when it comes in. The towns in the Delta will be a while in rebuilding most of them have sections about one quarter of the town burned to the ground by V.C. and bomb strikes etc to regain towns from the V.C. We have been resupplying many of the towns. As we go in often there are snipers on the roof tops but most of the towns are mopping up now and should be normal pretty soon. There has been lots of action. I have been here 1½ months already and the time is passing very quickly. I don't need anything. I could go without the last few weeks but we always have something like that to contend with. It makes life challenging.

> So long.
> I will write in another week.
> Hi to Nana and Uncle Fred. Love,
> Your Son, Fred

We picked up a full load of anti-tank rockets at Bien Hoa Air Base near Saigon and were delivering them to Bac Lieu Airfield, deep in the Delta. It was a heavy load for a D model Huey, and as we arrived overhead of the destination airfield and started our approach from altitude, the damn engine quit. I was the co-pilot and Charlie Hardin was the aircraft commander. We had a door gunner and crew chief on board, as was standard practice with us. Charlie lowered the collective and began an autorotation heading for the airfield at Bac Lieu. I called in, just as I had rehearsed, in as low and controlled a voice as I could muster: "Mayday, Mayday, this is Tiger 673 with an engine failure over Bac Lieu in Four Corps."

The controller on the other end amped up his voice and asked if we

There were two platoons of transport helicopters in our company: the Blue Tigers and the White Tigers. The third platoon, the Vikings, was our gunship platoon. Each platoon leader worked at creating an identity and esprit de corps among the pilots and enlisted flight crewmembers of their platoon. There was little room for traditional military protocols in the combat environment. Some crew chiefs and door gunners were given flight instruction by their aircraft commanders in case the pilots up front were incapacitated so that a flight crewmember was capable of flying the aircraft back to the base or at least getting it on the ground in one piece during an emergency or combat situation.

had everything under control. We were approaching touchdown. I don't know why, but I responded, "No sweat!"

We were lined up for the runway, but there was a big garbage dump off the approach end and with the heavy load of explosives we were sinking, and it looked like we were going to end up in the dump. That would not have been a good thing because the dump was full of old equipment and derelict vehicles and the helicopter was full of anti-tank explosives. So Charlie pulled a little pitch back in the blades to get us over the dump and we ran out of pitch at the bottom to cushion us on and just sort of fell in from about the last five feet. We hit the runway with a pretty good force that smashed the landing gear up into the undercarriage of the aircraft. We all exited the broken bird posthaste, in no hurry to stay in case of a fire. The next thing I remember I was standing about 100 feet away from the wrecked chopper looking back at what had previously been our trusted transportation and now looked like a pitiful off-kilter grasshopper. The skids got pushed up into the undercarriage, but the anti-tank weapons did not go off and no post-crash fire.

*   *   *

I recall that an early mission when I first started out as an FNG Peter Pilot was a resupply mission into an outpost deep in the Delta that had a lot of history of being a lone outpost of regular Vietnamese citizen soldiers led by a Catholic priest named Father Hoa. The triangular piece of dirt they defended was part of a "hamlet program" of the South Vietnamese government, establishing outposts designed in a triangle, rectangle or square configuration surrounded by a dirt mounded barrier with minefields and concertina wire. The outpost was located on a fork in a canal on a river and was surrounded by dense jungle and known as bad guy territory outside of the wire. My aircraft commander was Chief Warrant Officer Vic Beaver, a warrant officer we called Beaver because of his last name and the family TV show *Leave It to Beaver* that was popular in our youth. Later, after his tour in Vietnam, he wrote a very good novel, *Sky Soldiers*, reflective of our experiences in the 121st Assault Helicopter Company at Soc Trang.

We picked up our ash and trash at Ca Mau and headed further south towards the outpost indicated on the map as Nam Can. From altitude, everything south of Ca Mau was lush green jungle canopy. It had an ominous feeling about it, and pilots develop almost a sixth sense about places where things can go south in a hurry. This was one.

We arrived at our destination 15 kilometers south of Ca Mau. From the air it looked like a triangle piece of dirt about the area of a football field. Two sides of the compound were bounded by canals that widened when two tributaries joined at the south end of the compound. A berm was piled up outside the compound and on top of the berm was concertina wire. Between the berm and the water's edge was an area that was heavily mined, according to the Beaver, who had been in here before on resupply missions. When you're heavy and coming in or out of these places, you want to know where the minefields are and avoid them or it could be your last flight. Landing in a minefield is not conducive to longevity.

Vic told the crew to get ready and be on their guns. He'd been in here before, and the local VC usually sharpened their aim by taking a few shots at any helicopter on approach. Then he turned to me and said, "Mac, we approach this place from the south side over the river and land on that little piece of dirt just inside the wire at the top of the triangle."

He keyed the mic and contacted the outpost and asked them to pop smoke to give us an idea of how the wind was blowing. Three different colors of smoke were visible shortly in the area. One was near the dirt landing area and two others, yellow and blue, were in small clearings outside of the outpost by a few hundred yards. These were our invitation from Charlie to land in the wrong place so that they could have us for lunch. Vic transmitted "Roger the red smoke," and got a couple of clicks reply on the radio.

He said, "Here we go!" He dumped the nose over into a corkscrewing descent down to about 30 feet above the river, about a quarter mile down the main confluence of the two canals to the south and we low-leveled up the river, slowing to about 60 knots. Then we heard a few pops and the distinct sound of a couple of them hitting the fuselage like a hammer. He hauled back on the cyclic and did a big flare and dropped into the dirt landing pad. The dust and debris flew everywhere, obscuring the pad from view for a few seconds. Then the dust settled and some local friendlies approached the helicopter, smiling under their metal helmets and flak jackets, and welcomed us into their version of the Alamo out here on the River of No Return. I looked at Vic, and he was as calm as could be.

As we shut the engine down, I said, "Was this normal?"

He answered, "Yeah, we hardly ever get into here without a little excitement. Outside of this dirt triangle, the VC own the jungle, but they don't mess around too much with Father Hoa because he knows so many people in this area. If we had had a gun team in the area, we might have asked them to fly cover for us, but this is how we do it when we are on our own."

I thought, "Man that was some wild-ass approach that no one ever taught us in flight school. Now we are a sitting duck if they decide to mortar us while we are shut down on the ground in this godforsaken place." I didn't look forward to the takeoff from here.

Vic said, "Let's get out and see how good a shots they were." We found a couple of bullet holes in the tail boom and fuselage but nothing critical was hit, just another opportunity for the contractors back at Soc Trang to use their metal patching skills.

Our takeoff consisted of pulling pitch in the unloaded bird, a pedal turn and charging down the river to 100 knots and then a cyclic climb back to altitude. The local VC must have either been eating their lunch or giving us a break because no fire was received on our departure. It was a good feeling to be out of there.

On a later mission during Tet, the Beaver spent a few days with his crew on the ground in another outpost, Tieu Can, after a similar resupply mission. Strategic shots from the enemy that time resulted in multiple leaks in the fuel tank and an ensuing attack on the outpost. They were required to hunker down in the outpost awaiting the arrival of a mission to pull them out and recover their aircraft. Things often were unpredictable on these missions resupplying remote and necessary outposts without the protection of a gunship cover.

* * *

When I made aircraft commander in slicks, I was assigned to be the designated pilot for a Vietnamese province chief, General Minh. He was called "Little Minh" to distinguish him from another General Minh, who was called "Big Minh." On days when assigned, I would be scheduled in a D model transport-type helicopter and would pick him up, sometimes with another Vietnamese officer or two, and we would fly him to one of the cities or to observe an operation, usually to confront some Viet Cong resistance.

Frequently, we would start early in the morning, and then land in a city that had been deemed secure enough for lunch, provided by some local supporter or associate, and then fly another mission in the afternoon around the province. On this particular day, we landed at a soccer field in the middle of My Tho. We were met by soldiers in ARVN jeeps and driven to a villa.

The meal started as usual with scented washcloths, served to us with silver tongs. This was followed by fish and vegetable courses, accompanied by orange pop, and ended with a type of cookie. The general introduced us to his hosts as "my number one pilot and his crew." As the meal came to a close, General Minh announced that he had "something special" for us.

With this statement he made a gesture with his hand. The French doors of the dining room opened and in walked 12 uniformed soldiers armed with AK-47s, B40 rocket launchers, Chi-com Mausers and other obviously Chinese Communist weapons. As the soldiers filed in and spaced themselves in military fashion equidistant around the walls of the formal dining room, with the weapons held at the ready, surrounding us on three sides, we shifted in our seats uncomfortably.

Without a word being spoken, I could see the collective concern in the faces of our crewmembers. Had we just been treated to the Last Supper and were we now to be the unwilling participants and recipients of a rerun of the classic movie of Al Capone and the Saint Valentine's Day Massacre? The fear in the room was palpable.

The general preempted further discomfort by announcing, "I have arranged for a display of captured weapons for my number one pilot and his crew." The crew and I, who shared a mutual discomfort, breathed a collective sigh of relief.

Each soldier stepped forward upon command from the general and presented arms, while the general described each captured weapon. He would take the weapon, clear the bolt, and point it out the doorway. Then he would elaborate on the recent operations in which the weapon was captured. He was obviously knowledgeable about the enemy's weapons and how they had been used against his own ARVN troops and seemed delighted to be able to demonstrate how to chamber rounds and sight each weapon. We were captivated by the honor of this demonstration being organized for us. As the final weapon was brought forward and demonstrated and the soldiers were ordered to proceed out of the room, I expressed to the general our deep appreciation for this thoughtful gesture and demonstration.

The missions I flew with General Minh were interesting and a welcome respite from the uncertainty of combat assaults. Usually they were what we would call VIP-type missions consisting of looking over the countryside in the province and checking on each town's leaders in his province and his soldiers in the field.

There were a couple of times when he was displeased with the loyalty of a city, town, or area, and would say over the intercom something like, "These people are not paying their taxes and are loyal to the VC. This is a free-fire zone." Of course, every flight crew knew that the words "free-fire zone" meant that any person sighted in the area described could be assumed to be enemy and could be engaged. My crew also knew that they had to have permission from the aircraft commander beyond this to fire weapons, to clear weapons, or to engage the enemy. Unless we were in a combat operation, or unless we were taking fire and they had been given the "cleared to fire" command, they were not to fire. I let the passing comments from the general be just that, and we did not engage the people we saw when he made these statements. He seemed unfazed by our inaction, so I guess he was just blowing smoke. Sometimes the area below us was obviously populated by people going about their daily business of rowing to market or farming. The unsettling part about this was that the permission he extended to us was legally the only permission a flight crew needed. I'm glad we had standard operating procedures and firing discipline built into our unit.

I enjoyed the variety, relationship, and missions that we had with General Minh. My crew and I had the opportunity to fly into the center of a number of cities in the Delta and to meet interesting political leaders and see where they worked and lived. It was a welcome counterpoint to combat assaults and ash-and-trash resupply missions. The flying was challenging in its own way because in the smaller cities we were avoiding structures and power lines and antennas as we landed in the heart of each town or city. It resulted in our being able to see and experience how the war was affecting those loyal to the government of South Vietnam in positions of power and leadership. The cultural norms and courtesies of the upper-echelon citizenry were on full display during our visits. We were welcomed into impressive villas. Associates interested in impressing their leader often rolled out the red carpet to him and to us as his flight crew. Lunches and dinners were in elegant dining rooms, and meals were served with china and crystal and utensils of bronze with black buffalo horn handles. Scented hand towels preceded each meal.

Soc Trang, Vietnam
Sunday, February 11, 1968

Dear Mom, Dad, Family,

Things are settling down a little but we're still on 24 hour alert. Most of the V.C. activity in our area has centered in a town to the South of us which might indicate that they are slowly moving back to the wooded areas in the south of the Delta where they are known to base their headquarters and supply stores. Their activities in the area, however, has been sufficient for us to remain ready 24 hrs a day.… As usual time is really moving. In 5 more days I'll have been here 2 months only 10 months to go. I now have about 325 hrs of flight time. Last night I flew flare ship for 10 hrs on airfield security dropping flares where movement is detected and generally being in the air in case of mortar attack or attempted ground assault. Tonight I am waiting for the mission board to be posted to find what tomorrow holds and which chopper I sleep in tonight.… I want to do something constructive in line with my talents and just have the time and opportunity to do some small things like go up in the mountains or fly. I think maybe my experience here would be useful and I feel a lot more ready to try for whatever I decide to do.

Love,
Your Son, Fred

Tet 1968: A Turning
Point in the War

The focus of the Tet Offensive of 1968 was a coordinated attack by the Viet Cong and the North Vietnamese on every military installation and civilian town or city in the country. Our airfield was attacked in a similar fashion, but due to the planning and preparation efforts our senior officers required, we were in a little better position to resist the attacks. We weren't as strategic a target as the larger fields of Vinh Long and Can Tho. The airfields of Can Tho and Vinh Long were secured within a matter of days of fighting, and among the disturbing findings were that the Viet Cong had maps of the fields and knew just what and who they were after. This was an indication that some of the Vietnamese people who worked on these bases from neighboring towns must have provided the hand-drawn maps and inside information to the VC.

In the first week of February 1968, the Tet Offensive was initiated by the Viet Cong and the North Vietnamese throughout Vietnam, and we were engaged in defending our own airfield. We heard that communications indicated that the perimeters had been breached at Vinh Long and Can Tho, two larger airfields than ours, and that officers and enlisted men had been killed in the attacks. At first, this sounded surreal to us, but as the first days unfolded, we began to realize that these were not just isolated incidents but part of a new major offensive in the war.

One of the missions I was a part of involved doing resupply missions into the city of My Tho in the first few days of Tet. These were memorable because we were sniped at from shooters on rooftops as we made these resupply runs and had to take their location into account when returning for additional resupply missions.

*　*　*

Another set of missions involved making combat assaults like we normally did in the outlying rice paddies or province cities of the Delta, but

These children are gathered around on what seems to be a soccer stadium look-
ing in awe at our helicopter. When we flew in with a Vietnamese leader to a unit
based in a city like My Tho or Can Tho we would often land in a courtyard, park
or athletic field. The visiting dignitary might be whisked off by car or jeep to
meet with influential city leaders and we would remain with the helicopter and
interact with the children. We enjoyed the banter back and forth. The children
would ask for candy, money, or cigarettes. We had to be very clear about them
keeping their distance from the helicopter for their own safety and because
some of them were tempted to steal knives, cameras, or C-rations if they were
left unattended.

what was different this time was we were making them at night into our
own airfields to take them back from the intruders. These particular missions seemed unreal because they were night missions, we were loaded with
combat troops, and the skies were lit up by flares and tracers being shot at
us by the enemy and from inside of the airfields by the enemy intruders.

In early January of 1968, I enrolled in an undergraduate correspon-
dence course from the University of Washington back home titled Modern
British Poetry. I read the assignments during downtime from flying missions and extra duty assignments and had received good marks on a couple of submissions. The Tet Offensive hit at the end of January 1968. During
Tet, as the fighting amped up and there was a coordinated effort throughout
the country to overthrow the South Vietnamese government and to turn
the tide of the war in favor of the Viet Cong and the North Vietnamese, our
lives changed. We had been flying long days and sleeping under the helicopters at night. They were distributed inside and around the edge of the

perimeter of the airfield to change their location from standard and to be ready to respond to either evacuate them from the airfield or involve them in missions of moving ARNV and/or Ninth Infantry American troops where needed. We were literally staying at the ready in these positions for a few days, and as we got up one morning to greet the new day, the aircraft commander Mike McNamara, an avid photographer, was taking pictures of the Air Force fighters putting in bomb runs just outside of our perimeter. I heard a swishing sound and then a couple more and asked Mike if he was rewinding his camera. He said, "Nope," and then we both hit the deck as we realized the sound was bullets whizzing overhead. They came from a sniper outside the perimeter who had us in his sights, despite his poor aim.

I completed my next assignment for my class, which I kept with me to work on when we had downtime between missions. I wanted to mail it in but knew the stamps were in my room and the post office was across the runway. As the shooting subsided, I ran across the runway to return to our hooch, got the stamp and put it on the letter, and turned it in to the post office before returning to our ship. All of this was done while we were under fire. Upon my return and a little reflection, I realized that this was absolutely crazy. I decided I better put this course on hold while we are involved in this level of activity. In this context, a course in Modern British Poetry is not worth risking my life in order to turn in assignments.

The Tet Offensive started for our airfield on January 31, 1968, in the wee hours of the morning. At about 3:00 a.m., we heard several loud explosions. This resulted in "scrambling" our gun team, the Vikings, for what seemed like a typical response to a mortar attack. Things remained quiet after the gun team launched, and the all-clear was ultimately sounded. Everyone left the bunkers where they had gone for cover and went back to their hooches. About an hour later, incoming mortars began to fall on the airfield. These were responded to with another gunships scramble. Then a third attack occurred. This led people to the conclusion that something different was happening.

The distinct sounds of gunfire were heard off in the distance towards the city of Soc Trang, and soldiers on guard duty around our perimeter began reporting small arms fire and bullets whistling overhead. Reports began coming in of skirmishes between ARVNs in the city of Soc Trang being confronted by attacking Viet Cong units. The Vikings were now on high alert and were engaged in providing gun cover and helping push back the offensive, as well as in responding to mortaring of our own airfield.

We were on the ground at this time awaiting our next assignments. All personnel not engaged in flight missions were assigned perimeter positions or some other combat-related role. There was an ominous feeling in the air that the war was taking on a new and more immediately threatening dimension. The next night, and for many thereafter, mortars were fired onto the airfield. At one point I remember hearing that the YO-3A glider had detected images of troops advancing towards the airfield perimeter in larger numbers. This was the time we all started wondering if we were going to get overrun and be involved in combat and hand-to-hand fighting against the VC.

Our Artillery Detachment was positioned in defense of the airfield, and they had a unique experience of Viet Cong soldiers breaking into a facility that was their base just outside of our perimeter to the north. Some of the artillerymen actually confronted them face to face. But to the artillerymen's amazement, the enemy soldiers seemed very young and confused about the surprise encounter and withdrew, and the nine men of the detachment quickly retreated back temporarily to safety inside Soc Trang Airfield.

On February 9, 1968, a little more than a week into the Tet Offensive, our gunships were engaged in resisting mortar attacks at Soc Trang and retaking infiltration situations at Vinh Long and Can Tho. The slicks were involved with resupplying outposts and strategic locations. White Tiger 782 went down by a place we called Five Canals for the juncture of those north and west of our airfield. The aircraft was not heard from as expected. An aircraft sent to check on where they had last been reported to be operating observed the crash site. It appeared that there were no survivors. On that aircraft were crewmembers we knew very well in various capacities and as friends.

The aircraft commander was Captain Franklin S. Bradley, who was credited with seeing that our perimeter defenses at Soc Trang were such that they withstood the unexpected Tet Offensive attacks better than other airfields. The pilot was Warrant Officer Ricky Lee Hull. He was a personal friend of mine, and I had been teaching him some guitar chords for singing in the Tigers' Den. The crew chief was SP5 Paul R. Anzelone, and the door gunner was SP4 Michael Lynch. Apparently, the aircraft had been shot down, and there was evidence of a fire.

Back at Soc Trang on another occasion during the first few days of Tet, the word circulated that a Viking ship had been hit with gunfire and the AC Larry MacDonald had been wounded. We went out to the flight line to watch for the incoming gunships. I remember seeing the medical personnel out on the flight line, and as the gunship landed the crew reclined the armor-plated seat back and pulled Mac out through the cargo door area. Personnel from our clinic were there to meet the incoming gunship and took him into the field hospital area. It was one of the times that he was awarded a Purple Heart for his wounds. He was one stoic cookie and a cool customer under fire.

We believed we were in the best aviation unit in the U.S. Army in Vietnam. Our company area entrance and our stationery proclaimed us "The World Famous Soc Trang Tigers." There was an unstated expectation that we did not turn down missions. We had a reputation to uphold, and many units told us they counted on us to get the job done. Before our time in 1967–1968 the company had an actual captured tiger mascot in a cage in the company area.

Soc Trang, Vietnam
Wednesday, February 21, 1968

Dear Nana and Family,

... Things are still pretty hot. We got mortared the last two nights in a row. I was flying the flare ship last night and as the first rounds hit we scrambled, dropped flares over the tubes, and the gunships blew the hell out of them with rockets. But the VC are pretty well fortified in earthen bunkers and it would take almost a direct hit with a 250 pounder to finish them off. We just keep pounding them and they go underground & come out again the next night to lob a few more in at us. We're still on full alert sleeping in the ships at night and have been since about 28 Jan when all this started (Tet Offensive). Our losses have not been very substantial but it sounds like Charlie is getting wailed on.

Anyway despite the long hours I'm feeling very well and getting a lot of flight time in so all is well.... I like what I am doing and the experience is invaluable. I take care and always have my PF flyers on when they yell "incoming."

Love, Cousin, Fred

8

Combat Assault Reality Therapy

Flying in general has been characterized by some aviation writers as hours of boredom punctuated with seconds of stark terror. I would say, based on my experiences, that military helicopter flying during combat assaults in Vietnam in the IV Corps area of the Mekong Delta was characterized by hours of excitement and uncertainty punctuated regularly by minutes of stark terror, adrenaline rush, and sometimes undesired resultant experiences. Combat assaults were the meat and potatoes of what we did many days in our role as slick drivers. A combat assault for our company usually consisted of from three to nine transport helicopters flying in formation, escorted by a light (two helicopters) or heavy (three helicopters) team of gunships. The whole operation was coordinated and overseen by a command and control helicopter overhead at 1,000 feet. There were frequently other aircraft involved in preparing the landing zone. One was a forward air controller from our airfield with the call sign "Shotgun." They flew a light plane with rockets to mark targets or suspected targets either for fighter aircraft, artillery, or gunships. The FAC was a high-risk role in a relatively unarmed small airplane to guide the bombing or artillery in advance of the combat assault. These preparation bombings or artillery barrages were optional and used when there was reason to believe that the landing zone would be "hot" with active resistance and groundfire.

The transport helicopters we flew in 1967 and 1968 were initially D model Hueys that were replaced in the middle of my tour with more powerful H model Hueys. They looked essentially the same but had a larger engine. They were one of the most resilient aircraft in the Army's inventory, and at the same time they were vulnerable to groundfire and limited in the protection they provide their pilots and crew. The capacity of the slick was either six to eight American combat-ready infantry soldiers or 10 to 12 Army of the Republic of Vietnam combat-ready soldiers. The difference being in the size of each.

*   *   *

When you are an aircraft commander in a slick flying in formation on a combat assault you are focused. Formation flying is an all-consuming activity. The basic formations we used were straight trail, staggered trail, echelon right, echelon left, and Vs of three, As the pilot on the controls you are concentrating your whole being on your sight picture, which is a spot on the aircraft next to you and in front of you that is your reference point while your hands and feet make subtle adjustments to the pedals, cyclic, and collective to stay in the slot you are in. Changing formation to another requires clear understanding on the part of each aircraft commander of his current position and what he will do when given a predetermined signal to move into the next position. Your rotor blades are almost overlapping your reference aircraft and you are aware of not letting the aircraft move in too close or out too far. You are not looking anywhere but at that aircraft you are flying off of. You know that your other pilot is checking the gauges and ready to take the controls if you get hit. Your ears are tuned in to hear the commands on the radio, from Tiger Lead, the pilot and crewmembers in your ship, and the aircraft commanders in the other ships in formation.

"Tiger Lead is RP 5 inbound with smoke."

"Roger lead, Viking 23, stumps and water in the LZ, light fire received from North tree line, call fire, suggest minimal down time, south east departure, avoid overflying the tree line at your 12, will be right with you all the way in and out."

"Tigers, tighten up, call fire, pick your spot, call when up."

"Tiger 5 receiving fire, 3 o'clock."

"Tiger 3 taking hits 090 north tree line."

"Tiger lead, pacs off, pulling pitch, Left 200."

"Two is up."

"Three is up, light fire 045 from hooch."

"Four is up, guy in black by hooch with a weapon."

"Five is taking automatic weapons fire, heading 045, small hooch 50 yards."

"Viking 24 is rolling in on the hooch, rockets and minis. Hang in there, 5 we are with you."

"Six is up, taking hits, gauges are holding."

"Seven is taking fire."

"Eight is up."

"Nine is up, lead your flight is up. Nine is taking small arms fire from the hooches."

"Twenty-three, Tiger Lead, thanks for the cover, stay with us."

"Lead, 23, will do—24 how's it look on your side?"

"Twenty-four is dumping on the hooches and the north tree line and staying tight on the Tigers, all are currently up."

"Lead, 23, your flight looks good, we will follow you out and cover the ground troops."

The crew chief and door gunner are calling fire received and the fire they are initiating for your information. They don't have time at that point to ask for permission to fire. You have given them instructions on approach, and they make the decisions at this point and you live with them.

Miscarriage

They laid her roughly in the helicopter
The sergeant in the back was joking over the intercom that she
   could always walk to the hospital. Her twisted form under
   the blanket convulsed and an expression of fear and pain shot
   across her countenance, but she remained silent. She just had
   a miscarriage and was hemorrhaging badly.
"These slopes are all alike," he said. "Just like animals. You have
   to treat them like that. Ha Ha. Well just the other day …."
The miles crept by slowly, the blades popping steadily overhead.

Shut your mouth cried out within me
as my lips formed the word "why"?

Soc Trang, Vietnam
Saturday, March 16, 1968

Dear Mom, Dad, and Family,

…my name is on the list to get in the Vikings—gunship platoon of the 121st, so I think now it is just a matter of time. Their requirements are fairly rigid for you have to have quicker reactions flying low-level and they take a few more chances, but that type of flying really appeals to me. So I am hoping to have a check ride in a few weeks for it. I will keep you informed about what turns up. The food isn't really too bad.

Today I'm Airfield Officer of the Day. That means I am up all-night and responsible for checking all the bunkers on the perimeter to ensure communications and everything under control, also general security of the Airfield. It's a job that is rotated and you have it about every two months. Everything here is running as usual and not much out of the ordinary.

So long for now. Love
Your Son, Fred

Soc Trang, Vietnam
Friday, March 29, 1968

Dear Mom Dad & Family,

Well today I ought to thank my lucky stars a little anyway. We had an engine failure at 3000' yesterday. We got it on the ground OK but wrapped it up pretty well. Everyone escaped without injury and we were over a secure area when it happened so it all goes chalked up to more war stories. Other than that no more news. Same old everyday missions…. Things are calming down here. The weather is getting more humid with the approach of the wet season.

Love
Your Son, Fred

The Hooch Maid

How quietly she cleans the room
Deftly wielding the bamboo broom
Gently she dusts the writing table
Small she is and yet how able
And willing to do the small things right
To clean diligently the overhead light
And only a fool could fail to see
The beauty in her simplicity.

The women who did our laundry, cleaned our rooms, changed our sheets, and polished our boots were from the nearby city of Soc Trang. Every day they would walk through the entry gate past the military police that guarded our entrance and would come to our area and collect our clothes and take them to be hand-washed. These women worked for very little pay and always approached their work with smiles on their faces and peaceful demeanors. They reminded us about the dignity of work and doing even the humblest of tasks in a thorough and diligent manner.

Soc Trang, Vietnam
Sunday, April 7, 1968

Mom, Dad, and Family,

...we flew today in a ship with inoperative fuel gauges and sporadic boost fuel pumps. To make a long story short due to a communication issue with the aircraft commander, a monsoon storm, and a poor aircraft we almost ran out of fuel right on the Cambodian border, in the middle of a torrential rain and we weren't sure of our exact location. Anyway tonight I'm back at Soc Trang safe and sound.

There was a peaceful comradery among the many women who did the house-cleaning and laundry work on our base. They worked as a team and coordinated the tasks they accomplished. We were aware of their attention to detail and the way our clothing and artifacts were respected and kept in order. There was an overriding sense of trust and responsibility that characterized their work for us.

> About the bombing cutback, we haven't felt any repercussions here in the Delta and I doubt if it will have much effect on the over-all situation here. I talked to the platoon leader of the gunships again and they will have a few openings next month, so I will keep you posted. I broke 500 hours in country last week so I am well on the way towards a goodly number for my tour.
>
> Everything is going fine. Love,
Your son, Fred

*   *   *

One day, when walking by a hangar on the other side of the tower, I noticed the door slide open to reveal what looked like a large glider painted in camouflage with a three-bladed propeller and a muffler pipe that ran from the engine in the nose all the way back along the fuselage. "Whoaaa. This is some kind of top secret aircraft!" was my thought process. Below the aircraft was slung a basketball-like fixture attached to the undercarriage. It had a bubble canopy over the cockpit and turned out to be a limited-edition glider called a YO-3A that was used to monitor troop movements. It was equipped with an electronic device that detected human urine from the air with an infrared detection device and was used to identify where enemy troops were concentrated.

Initially it was hangared at Soc Trang, kept under wraps during the day, and only taken out at night to fly. The pilot and an observer were tasked with flying the aircraft quietly over enemy territory, observing activity, and reporting it. When the Tet Offensive of 1968 occurred, during the initial days of the attacks on bases throughout the country, there was a report from one of these aircraft that had detected a significant number of people advancing towards our airfield. That was a little bit unsettling as we envisioned being overrun by Viet Cong.

There was some probing and infiltration of our base but not to the extent that occurred at other Delta airfields where perimeters were breached, positions were taken, and personnel were killed.

We were up on night patrol one particularly dark moonless night, flying mortar patrol with a light gun team, when a black form passed underneath us by about 500 feet, lights off, unannounced. We called the tower and were then informed that it was an aircraft on an approved mission. It turned out to be the YO-3A.

Soc Trang, Vietnam
Tuesday, April 30, 1968

Dear Mom, Dad, and Family,

… We have been busy lately. I am an aircraft commander now responsible for the helicopter, crew, and for teaching a new pilot from my experience flying here in the Delta. I also am really involved trying to keep this newspaper organized and out on time. It seems like everyone enjoys reading about what's happening in the company but no one has any time to contribute articles for it. The wet season is here. When it rains it really comes down. The mud gets a foot deep in a matter of minutes. But the showers usually pass as quickly and unexpectedly as they come, so they are usually fairly easy to circumnavigate. And when the sun comes out again it's usually very sticky and humid.

Temperatures lately have been reaching the high 90s in the afternoon. Thinking of you often,

Love, Your Son, Fred

Made in the Image and Likeness

Hey God!
Are you there?
In that man with the long black hair?
With the dirty hands and face?
Does he really live in that filthy place?
Does he know you?
Not like I do.
Does he have to?
I don't think so.

Soc Trang, Vietnam
May 14, 1968

Dear Mom, Dad, and Family,

    … You asked about our command structure. Flying here depends on experience more than rank. Regardless of rank, you fly pilot with an experienced aircraft commander who shows you the ins and outs of the Delta, the weather, navigation, and particularly the enemy situation. There are places you resupply where you know you will receive fire and there are certain ways to approach to provide the least exposure. The aircraft commander is responsible in all situations for the aircraft, mission, pilot, and crew. It is his prerogative and decision to accept a certain mission or not depending on whether he thinks the cause merits excessive exposure to the safety of the crew and aircraft. The Tigers have a reputation here in the Delta for getting the job done. So almost always we'll give it a shot. If the fire gets too intense, the a/c makes the go/no go decision. Most of our ships look like marvels of sheet metal patching anyway, so we try to keep hits at a minimum. Besides bullets aren't conducive to longevity. I'm an aircraft commander in transports and have been for three weeks. Now that I have the experience with loads and a fairly good knowledge of the IV Corps area I am trying to get into gunships. I should have some word in the next couple of weeks. Well 5 months down and only 7 to go. Have over 600 combat hours. I've been scared many times. I still really enjoy the flying and I am learning more every day. I hope you are all well as I am in fine health.

    There is still much more to see.

Love,
Your son, Fred

Why Him and Not Me?

A man
With a long pole
Scrounges around in the hole
We throw our refuse in
Looking for a scrap of meat
Or some worn out shoes for his blistered feet
Or just a damn piece of garbage to eat.
Why him and not me?

God, what should my life be?

Soc Trang, Vietnam
May 16, 1968

Dear Nan & Harnishes & Uncle Fred,

    …between a lot of flying and writing the company newspaper I'm really pressed for time. Thanks Nan for the most recent letter and news of the relatives around Tacoma. Now we are in the wet season and the monsoon rains are really something else. Charlie still manages to put a few holes in our flying machines but no major action lately and it keeps the sheet metal people busy. I'm in fine health. 5 months down and 7 months to go. Thanks again for the letters and hello to all in Tacoma.

Love,
Your Grandson,
Fred

9

Stayin' Alive in Soc Trang

The Tigers' Den was our airfield's officers' club. It was a structure right out of an Orient Express movie set. The walls were bamboo and wood. The ceiling was thatched. There were overhead fans that lazily turned around and blew the humid air over the customers. Large red hand pump fire extinguishers were in four of the corners. The floor was tile. The bar was in an L shape and would seat about 15 people. There were also tables and chairs throughout and some booths as well. It was shared by officers from three primary units: the 121st Assault Helicopter Company (the Soc Trang Tigers Slicks and the Vikings Gun Platoon), the 33rd Maintenance Detachment (the Wrecker and other retrieval aircraft), and the 85th Medical Detachment (Dustoff 85 and 87). We also had a doctor, a dentist, air traffic control tower operators, military police officers, engineers, artillery, military police, and command and control personnel on our airfield.

The Tigers' Den was the refuge and gathering place for the warrant officers, lieutenants, captains, and majors who did the flying. Occasionally the commanding officer came through. When he did, those inside came to attention and were usually instructed to be at ease if it was just a social call. Once in a great while, if there was a problem of epic proportions, the presence of the commander might signal that enough damage and destruction had been inflicted for one evening, but this rarely happened.

Our days were sometimes very long, and that sometimes involved 14 hours of flying, shooting, being shot at, and other various forms of entertainment and excitement. Sometimes emergency lights came on during short final into a hot LZ, bullets came through the fuselage, people screamed on the radio "I'm taking hits" or "we're losing altitude" or the dreaded "going down in the LZ," followed by absolute quiet when the engine quit running. Even just a day of standby at a remote staging field and the ultimate cancellation of a mission for weather or lack of contact could be exhausting.

We often sang in the Tigers' Den after a long day of difficult missions. The singing followed a ritual pattern of progressively escalating behavior that culminated with the songs and even some unique post singing activity if the day was particularly conflicted. One example was the slip-and-slide contest. Someone would buy up cans of the least desired beer and pour them into the hand pump fire extinguishers. Then the floor and some of the patrons were hosed down with rigorous pumping, the furniture was moved, and a few brave souls fortified with Vitamin B or a B52 (shot glass of bourbon dropped into a glass of beer) would take a running start and slide across the beer slicked floor into the bar amidst raucous countdown, cheers, and laughter.

The songs were rude, crude, and fall-down-on-your-face funny, at least to us in the context of being at war. We all knew the verses, and the points of emphasis were always made with a rousing chorus. They were filled with obscene language and sexually charged phrases, alliteration, and assonance, and they were, in our collective opinion, a great way to bring to closure the craziness of a day spent in-country.

So when we came into the place, it was somewhat like the media images of some early Western movies and the shootouts at the local saloon. Sometimes after just a few drinks, tuned up gun drivers would say something like, "It's time to throw the slick drivers out of here!" The Tigers would play along to humor them and then re-enter to the cheers of other Tigers in the bar. It was all usually done in a good-natured atmosphere. The former sergeants who ran the bar and the local Vietnamese girls who waited on us were always in fine form and enjoyed the stories and the characters who told them.

I remember one particular night when we were in the Tigers' Den. Into our inner sanctum walked three gundrivers from the neighboring gun team called the Thunderbirds. We disrespectfully referred to them as the "Blunderbirds," but I'm sure they had their own derogative terms for us as well. These pilots were already pretty well tuned up and announced that they had just walked by the Viking flight line on their way into the club: "By the way, we just pissed on your aircraft."

We didn't know if this was true or not, but it was enough provocation for a couple of Vikings to leave the bar and return with some palm branches they had cut down off banana trees on the "Blunderbirds" flight line. They proceeded to run the branches through the overhead fans, and they were thrown all over the Tigers' Den to the cheers of all Tigers and Vikings present.

We flew a number of joint missions with the Thunderbirds gun teams and their Warrior slicks from the 336th AVN Company from Soc Trang and always worked well together in combat. This friendly rivalry created an atmosphere of competition that was, for the most part, a healthy factor in the combat environment.

10

Sisters, Orphans, POWs, and a Hospital

I was asked to report to the commander's office one day, and he asked me if I would be the assistant civic actions officer for the company. He explained to me that the 121st had a relationship with three social service-type programs in the city of Soc Trang, that he had asked the operations officer to take the lead in this responsibility area but that he needed an assistant in these duties, and that he had decided I would be the best person for this job. The three programs were in three different locations off base in town and involved a Catholic orphanage, a hospital, and a Chieu Hoi Center for retraining Vietnamese young men who had been involved with the Viet Cong and were now being reoriented towards the government of South Vietnam. It sounded like interesting work. My role was to coordinate with our support services and to see what sorts of humanitarian aid we could solicit from surplus food or supplies on our base and from friends and relatives back home to help these organizations. I was to accompany the operations officer in a jeep to town and to check in on these programs and then a couple of times a month see what we could do for them. The relationship with the orphanage and hospital had been started a few years earlier by one of the doctors at Soc Trang.

The orphanage population seemed like around 50 to 100 children from infants to school-aged children, and there were about five or six sisters on the staff. Their orphanage was in an old French villa and the sisters were a French order including older sisters from France and younger sisters who had joined the order from the local area. They wore white traditional nuns' habits and were very kind and dedicated. When I first visited the infant section, I was surprised to see how many young infants were being taken care of, and the conditions were pretty primitive. I think there were about 15 in a ward. Each had a bassinet they were in and many appeared sick, some with deformities. The babies appeared to be well taken care of, but there were flies around in the ward, and it seemed like a continuous activity to keep them from the babies. Sister Martha was introduced to me as the mother superior of the sisters. She explained to me that in Vietnam at the time, if your baby was born with deformities, they were often abandoned or left for care with the sisters. She told me that generally the Viet Cong left their orphanage alone because it was the only hope for these children, and they seemed to respect the work being done by the sisters in the community. Back at the base the operations officer went around with me to our kitchen, medical clinic, PX, supply, motor pool, etc., and introduced me and explained our mission. Then he pretty well left me to coordinate with them and check in with them regularly to see if they had supplies that could benefit one of these

One of my duties as assistant and later acting civic actions officer was to organize picnics for the sisters and orphans from the Soc Trang orphanage. We would hold these picnics on a grassy area between the Vikings' hooches and operations. We had 50-gallon oil drums that were cut in half and supported with legs welded on in the maintenance shop for our barbecues. The sisters and children were brought out to the airfield in deuce-and-a-half trucks by our motor pool drivers. We cooked hamburgers, steaks, and hot dogs and had baked beans, chips, ice cream, soda pop, beer and a cake made and served by our cooks for these occasions. The civilian contractors joined us. The orphans wore little seersucker suits and dresses. We all enjoyed carrying them around, singing songs with them, playing games, and giving presents. It was a real connection with family and home for many. We played baseball and volleyball and the sisters were delighted to share in the games and festivities.

This is a picture of our company jeep parked outside of the orphanage in downtown Soc Trang. The orphanage was staffed by a mother superior from France and French and Vietnamese sisters. One of my "extra duties as assigned" was to be assistant civic actions officer and to provide supplies and assistance to this orphanage, a hospital, and a Chieu Hoi (POW retraining facility) in the town of Soc Trang. We brought some of the orphans and sisters out to the airfield for barbecues and picnics from time to time. We also asked our relatives and friends back home to send us clothing and medical supplies for the orphans. We were touched by the primitive conditions and the way these women took in the abandoned and orphaned children and took care of them. We were inspired by the positive attitude of the children and their warmth and laughter in spite of the on-going war.

organizations. We would then make runs into town with a jeep or truck and deliver the supplies.

We brought some of the sisters and some of the orphans out on a few occasions to the airfield in one of our trucks and had a barbecue for them. We entertained them on the grassy area in front of our hooch where we sometimes played games like volleyball. I played guitar and we sang simple children's songs and played games like softball and football with them. It was inspiring to see the interaction between the flight crewmembers and the contractors who said they were reminded of their own families back home. I began including information about these programs in my letters home, and my former seminarian friends and my mother and her friends gathered together money, medical supplies, and clothing that was sent to me for distribution to them. Our various support services and medical clinic provided surplus medicines, etc. from time to time. It was very rewarding work. Once following a barbecue and the delivery of medicine and clothing, Sister Martha gave me a goat that I brought back to the flight line. I didn't feel right saying "no thank you," and it was a very generous gesture from them, but we had to realize we were not equipped to have a goat running round the flight line and so we returned it on a subsequent trip.

The hospital was filled with Vietnamese men who had been wounded or were sick from their combat experiences. They were soldiers with the

A war involves everyone in the country in some form or another. This picture of one of our picnic/barbecues reminds me of the kindness and patience of the sisters in being there for these forgotten children. One of the small boys has left his crutches aside and is enjoying lunch with his friends. The children were very respectful and happy to be in a safe place enjoying the kinds of food and treats that children appreciate everywhere. Even these orphaned children were on their best behavior and demonstrated the manners and respect that the sisters exemplified in their prayer life and in exercising their nursing and teaching duties. Some of the soldiers are in their military uniforms signaling the ever-readiness of an assault helicopter company. Many of us who were not on duty at the time of these gatherings chose to wear civilian clothes. We were reminded in these settings of the many blessings in our lives while at the same time being aware of the high price being paid by so many in fighting this war.

This picnic picture shows the orphans surrounded by some of the care packages that had arrived from family and friends in America. Men in uniform are holding up children and being reminded of their own families back home. There is a soccer ball by one girl's feet. So many times, we would see children in hamlets and villages playing soccer on dirt fields, in alleyways, and in open fields. The Viet Cong attacked many of the houses and businesses in Soc Trang during the Tet Offensive of 1968, but they seemed to respect this orphanage and the work of the sisters.

Army of the Republic of Vietnam. I would go from bed to bed with a doctor or nurse, distribute small gifts of toiletries, etc., and shake their hands. They were very grateful for the simplest of gifts or supplies. I could see in their eyes the fear of the experiences they had been through and could see the various injuries they had experienced. Here again the hospital was clean and the nurses and doctors there were dedicated, but the conditions were primitive and anything we could provide was deeply appreciated.

The Chieu Hoi Center was like a primitive school setting where a number of young men were in classes for part of the day and were basically in a holding center the other parts of the day. Here we delivered supplies and clothing that were appreciated and were invited to look in at classroom settings where they were being instructed. This Chieu Hoi Center was certainly a more humane way to treat captured prisoners of war from the local community. I always came back from these visits feeling very grateful for my own life in America and motivated to do what I could to gather meager supplies and clothing for future visits. I doubt if anyone outside of the military would have known that when pilots and flight crewmembers were not piloting combat helicopters, they were engaged in this type of humanitarian work, but this is a reality and important work that goes on virtually anywhere a military operation is undertaken by the United States.

11

Helicopter Gunships

I was getting to know the Delta and the ins and outs of flying the D model Huey in the combat environment, and we were starting to get a few of the more powerful H models to replace them in the company. We had experienced the Tet Offensive of 1968. We had seen the loss of the momentum and the gradual tapering off of intermittent mortar attacks and the successful rebuilding of the airfields and cities. Combat assaults had become a regular part of my schedule as well as flying General Minh around the province. It was the five-month marker in my 12-month tour. Mortar attacks were a regular occurrence, and we were seeing the rotation home of the pilots that trained us. We were welcoming new pilots and crewmembers into the unit and training them in the standard operating procedures of the unit.

One night, I had turned in a little early after a long day of combat assault missions and a couple of drinks in the Tigers' Den. The screen door of my room swung open, and in the faint light of the hallway I noticed six men had come in my sparsely furnished home room and were dressed in jungle fatigues, black T-shirts, and black berets.

"You better get up, McCarthy" was the introduction I recognized in my friend Jim's voice from the back of the group.

Another Viking started out, "We have come to tell you that we have decided that you will no longer be a Tiger but have been selected to be a Viking." The Vikings was the name of our gunship platoon. Our transport helicopters or slicks were divided into two platoons, the Blue Tigers and the White Tigers. It was a common practice in assault helicopter companies for a pilot new to Vietnam to fly slicks first, and then some were selected to be gunship pilots. Flying a gunship was considered an honor, and most pilots selected were honored by the selection. A pilot who joined the Vikings could choose at any time to return to flying slicks.

I think I said something like, "Gee, that's great," and shook everybody's hand while I was thinking a whole lot of disconnected stuff at the same time. Things like, "Holy crap ... these guys get shot at every day ... they scramble when there is a mortar attack ... and others head for the bunkers.... I have a fairly sweet deal flying a Vietnamese general around.... I have had being a gunship pilot as my goal from the early days of flight school.... This is my dream come true! ... I can do this.... I think! ...."

One pilot stepped forward with a black beret. Another handed me two black T-shirts with the instructions, "This is what we wear ... and by the way, you don't fly anything but gunships from now on." Though this whole process appeared to be a spontaneous activity, it was actually the culmination of a multi-step process. It had to be discussed in the platoon and cleared with the commanding officer of the 121st Assault Helicopter Company, and the platoon leader of the Blue Tigers as well as the Viking platoon leader would have had input prior to selection and this action being taken. Also the Vikings would have a pretty good idea that the pilot selected would say "yes" prior to this kind of a visit.

After the brief presentation they left—except for Jim. He was smiling and I asked, "Why did they pick me?"

Beautiful women have inspired aviators since the dawn of aviation. Many call their aircraft "her." "Hanoi Hannah" was a North Vietnamese radio personality along the lines of World War II propaganda deliverers, all of them called Tokyo Rose. On the airways Hannah taunted the Vikings, threatened them, and called them "those Blue Diamond Devils of the Delta." We had little question from her threats of what would happen to us if they captured us after raining down so much firepower on the enemy.

His response was, "I need a wingman I can trust."

I followed with, "What do I say if they assign me to fly slicks?"

Jim said, "They won't. They already know about this. If someone asks you to fly ash-and-trash, tell them to go to hell. You are a Viking!"

The sound of incoming rounds is very distinct ... you never forget it. First you hear a muted thud when they leave the tubes. Then the siren warns you that the flashes have been seen in the tower. A few seconds later, all hell breaks loose and the mortars start impacting all around.

I ran down the hallway in the Viking quarters as fast as I could and hit my knee on the screen door, tripped and fell flat on my face; but I got right up and kept going. I pushed open the swinging screen door and a mortar exploded in front of me out beyond the flight line. I hesitated a second, thought about turning around, and then ran again towards the gunship revetments.

The blade was untied from the tailskid by the crew chief, who held the right cockpit door open. I jumped in the right seat, turned on the overhead master, and pulled the starter trigger while the chief pulled out the seat armor along my right side. Then started what felt like the longest minute of my life ... while the turbine spooled up from dead silence to 6600 rpm. The VC were walking the mortars right down the flight line and into some of the buildings. By now, the other base personnel were in the bunkers with their heads down waiting for those of us in "the guns" to get airborne and get them to knock this shit off. The cockpit instruments were dull red and the dials were gradually coming to life. The distinctive smell of JP 4 igniting was filling the cockpit. The haze of mortars and gunpowder was hanging in the air.

I was careful about how quickly I rolled on the throttle so I didn't over speed the turbine or exceed the red line on the exhaust gas temperature gauge. While rolling on the throttle, the momentum from turning rotors causes the ship to rock from side to side. The accuracy of their mortars was mixed. Their aim was all over the place, sometimes erratic as hell with shells impacting within a block, or somewhere on the other company flight line or a building away, then one right behind us. The co-pilot began strapping in. We're coming up. The skids start sliding on the tarmac and we angle towards the runway. The skids scrape the asphalt ever so slightly with the weight of a fully loaded B model prior to translational lift. Sparks are flying from the skids dragging the runway, then the blades grab the air and pull the whole shaking metal conglomeration of bad-ass firepower into forward flight.

"Two-three is airborne, going hot. Directions tower?" My eyes and head are moving ... looking for flashing tubes....

"Mac 10:30 low trees along the canal just to the west of the perimeter. Rolling in ... hose 'em with the minis" ... four rockets away.

"Coming right," I announced on the intercom as I put the helicopter in a right turn. "Call out any more flashes!"

"None. No more, chief. We'll keep climbing and looking. Tower 23, flight of two Vikings circling west of the field on station. We'll stay airborne to see if these mothers have gone to bed for the night."

It is a clear beautiful night. The stars are out and so is the moon. We see clearly the dark foliage of the area we call the "Tiger's tail" of greenery that trails away to the south of the airfield along a creek into the darkness. The air is smooth and clear. It's deathly calm except for the whine of the engine and the whop whop syncopation of the blades. Our nav lights are off so we can't see 24 either. "24, this is 23. Anything happening north of Soc Trang?"

This is the view from behind the aircraft commander in the right seat and the pilot in the left seat looking out through the windscreen from the cockpit of a B model Huey Viking gunship. The inside of the cockpit feels like it is an extension of your body. After a few months in-country and a few hundred flight hours of missions you can tell the location of various switches, radios, controls, and circuit breakers just by feel. The helicopter feels like an extension of you and movements are seamless and intuitive. The sight in front of the aircraft commander is for the rockets. The sight in front of the pilot is for the mini guns. The radio communications are low-key, brief, and matter-of-fact. The operational area passes by in front of you at treetop level at 100 mph, and you are controlling the flight path with coordinated intuitive moves of all extremities... and then the enemy starts shooting at you!

Soc Trang, Vietnam
May 19, 1968

Dear Mom, Dad, and Family,

Well last night I was accepted into the armed platoon. That means no more flying transports. From now on until the end of my tour, I will fly B model gunships. I start flying night missions tonight with the Vikings. With the rains has come a marked increase in humidity and the days are getting pretty hot and sticky. I passed the 5-month mark 2 days ago, 7 months to go. I hope everything is going as well for all at home as it is for me here. I just don't have much other news, just that I got into guns and am looking forward to a whole new type of flying.

So Long for now. Love
Your Son, Fred

Sunset

It's evening....

The soft veil of an oriental night
Lingers in the frail silence
Of a warm day's failing light.

Just a moment, Then a whisper
And He puts the candle out.

Soc Trang, Vietnam
May 23, 1968

Dear Mom, Dad, and Family,

… I'm now in the gun platoon. I fly left seat and have a gun sight which controls 4 M-60 machine guns on flexible pylon mounts. The man flying right seat fires the rockets and does all the flying when we go down to tree top level. Then I just fire the machine guns and am there if he should get hit. There is much more to learn, a whole new type of flying and the aircraft commander has much responsibility for coordinating with transports on combat assaults and with the ground troops when they get in hot water and need some close fire support. It seemed like I knew the game as an aircraft commander in slicks but now I'm on the ground floor again as one of the new pilots in guns…. Now I will train to become an aircraft commander of a wing ship in a 2 ship fire team and eventually maybe a fire team leader if it turns out that I can catch on fast enough and have enough time left in country at that point. There are a few more tight situations to deal with and this offers a much greater challenge I think than slicks did. Will write again soon.

Love,
Your Son, Fred

Ode to Lieutenant Bill

(Parody of the Poem "Cremation of Sam McGee"
by Robert Service)

My co-pilot and I
Had been whooping it up

This is a view of the armament controlled by the pilots of a B model Huey gunship during 1968 in Vietnam. The seven rockets in the tubes on each pylon were
used in the Korean War. They were originally designed in the late 1940s. They
each had unfolding fins for accuracy that extended when they were fired and
were powered by a rocket motor. They were activated by a button on the side
of the aircraft commander's cyclic stick, and he had a pull-down sight in front
of him for sighting them on the target. The mini gun was a big advance over
the regular M60 and could fire up to the rate of 4,000 rounds per minute or
about 66 rounds per second. It makes an awesome sound when fired and literally obliterates a target. This gun was fired by the pilot with a trigger on the
cyclic control.

In the "Tigers' Den" Saloon
For quite a while
When we heard the incoming siren's tune

Whomp whomp was a familiar sound
As each of them exited their tubes
And before we knew it
The silence was shattered
And the mortars started falling to the ground

The men got up and they ran in fear out of their seats at the bar
And into the bunkers nearby leaving the Den door ajar

We knew we both were three sheets to the wind
And we knew that we had to scramble
And get a gunship up and rolling in
There wasn't any time to amble.

Cause if we didn't the shells would rain down harder on us all
And we could kiss our asses goodbye because
The destruction they brought would not be small
Seems like the only language Charlie understood
Was 2.75 rockets returning that night in the Soc Trang hood.

We charged out through the fusillade drunk as skunks could be
And fired up that tired old Model B and started to take off westerly
When scarcely out of the revetments
Bill squeezed the trigger on the mini gun
I tactfully leaned over and whacked him one
Saying we're not out of the revetment yet son.

The next day captain C said come here Mr Mac
Like there was something that only he knew
Turn around here by ops and see
the Mars antenna way up there
Do you have any idea
how it got so full of holes and air

No Sir, I don't, was my honest reply
Perhaps last night's mortar men hit it up high
They're getting more accurate every day
I said with a shrug and a sigh.
It looked to us both like a big round piece of metal Swiss cheese
With holes about the size of 7.62 if you please

Captain C said as we parted
I hope to hell it wasn't you
It wasn't, in all honesty I did reply but I couldn't help thinking it
    might have been Bill when he pulled that trigger on the fly

Strange things were done
In old Soc Trang, son
In those years that are gone by some of them made you laugh
And some of them made you cry

But the strangest night I do recall with a whimper and a sigh
Was that night filled with fate in 1968 when Bill and I scrambled
And lit up the Soc Trang sky.

> Soc Trang, Vietnam
> June 13, 1968

Dear Mom, Dad, and Family,

   Last night we worked airfield security at Can Tho 40 mi from here. We killed 3 vipers (snakes) on the line during the night—our crews had been sleeping on the ground between flights but that sort of ended the camp out. Altogether 7 were killed on the line; they are dredging for a new runway and that made them move up toward the present one.

   When we first went airborne the sky was lit up from tracers fire from about 20 different positions firing automatic weapons. It looked like a gun pilot's nightmare but proved to be Vietnamese outposts celebrating some holiday. A pretty quiet night— no mortars or obvious activity to speak of. We put in about 3 strikes where outposts recorded movement but received no fire in return. The time is beginning to drag a little but 4 more days and I'll hit the 6 month mark. Now have 750 combat hours about 1,000 total flight time counting flight training etc. Though it pours with the monsoon showers every afternoon, when the sun comes out the temp runs a fairly consistent 91 degrees. All in all everything is going fine. Gunships are a very different experience and to me a real challenge. Thanks again for the recent letters. Best to all.

Love,
Your Son, Fred

This is a picture of our Viking flight line at sunrise. Our gunships were right outside of our hooches so that we could scramble and be airborne in less than two minutes in the event of a mortar attack or priority mission. The parking spaces were called revetments and were built of 50-gallon drums filled with sand to protect the aircraft from flying shrapnel from the regular mortar attacks that occurred during our tour. We kept the Viking gunships "combat cocked." This meant that after refueling and regular maintenance, which often extended far into the night, a pilot would have gone through pages of a detailed preflight checklist down to the last two steps prior to starting the aircraft. When the siren went off indicating a mortar attack, all airfield personnel headed for a bunker but the Viking pilots and flight crewmembers, who would run out to the aircraft, switch on the ignition, pull the starter trigger and be up in the air a minute later to roll in with rockets on the tubes where the flashes were coming from. These attacks were among the most exciting and adrenaline-rushing combat experiences for a gunship crew. Sometimes they were pretty accurate and always they included trying to walk them down our flight line or into our quarters.

Soc Trang, Vietnam Thursday
13 June 68

Dear Mom & Dad,

I sent another letter today but I forgot to ask—please send one of my flight suits—I need one. We often have to "scramble" in case of mortar attack or downed aircraft in the middle of the night or when we are on free time & there is not enough time to put on a fatigue uniform. Thanks a lot please mail it soon.

Love, Your Son, Fred

Soc Trang, Vietnam Tuesday
June 25, 1968

Dear Mom, Dad, & Family,

...having a little trouble getting off this morning due to radio problems so I have a few minutes to get a note off. The situation here is carrying on about the same. We are working all over the Delta but lately a lot around Vinh Long and Can Tho.... We are mostly supporting ground operations and helping outposts that are under attack etc.

I wrote to a priest and some seminarians a few months ago when we were concerned with helping the many refugees from the January "Tet" offensive. From them I received almost $60, that was put to good use in an orphanage downtown run by Vietnamese Sisters of Providence. There are very many homeless children there and the sisters do a real good job despite the overcrowded conditions.

Of late everything is going well and I am in good health. I'm getting a little scruffier and more sunburned with the passing days. If it wasn't for an occasional scare or two I really enjoy the outdoor life and flying and am well adjusted to the climate. So thanks again for the letters and I am doing real fine.

Love,
Your Son and Brother
Fred

*   *   *

There are about a hundred switches and breakers on the instrument panel in a Huey, like a more complicated version of the dashboard of a car, and there are breakers and switches in an overhead panel as well. There are other switches and buttons in the cockpit and on the controls, and some are more consequential than others, as I would learn the hard way.

Flying a helicopter involves the use of all of one's extremities. Two fundamental controls affect the flight of a helicopter. There is a cyclic control that looks like a broomstick coming up from the floor between your legs, and it is moved so that the helicopter will move forward or backward and right and left. This control links to a swash plate that tilts the rotor system to bring this movement of the helicopter about.

Another control is called the collective, and it comes out of the floor on the left side of the pilot's and co-pilot's seats on an angle and, when moved, either puts pitch into the rotor blades or takes pitch out of the rotor blades. The resultant action is that the helicopter goes up when the collective is pulled up and down when the collective is moved in a downward motion at a hover or during a takeoff or landing.

The cyclic has a pistol grip type handle on it that includes a number of switches. Among the functions controlled through this handle are the radio, the trim, a cargo release, and the rockets when toggled on the instrument panel to fire.

I was flying wingman off another aircraft in what we call a light fire team, and the lead aircraft called receiving fire and that he was breaking right. I pressed what I thought was setting the stabilization system for a climb and shot a rocket right at the lead aircraft. For the first second my heart sank. I watched in horror thinking that the rocket might go right up the turbine tailpipe of the lead aircraft with catastrophic results including loss of the crew. The rocket dropped below the lead aircraft and exploded in the muddy rice paddy underneath him when it impacted the ground. Before I could disclose the mistake, the lead came on the radio and transmitted, "21 receiving heavier fire, might be a B-40 rocket."

I then keyed the mic and confessed something to the effect of, "21 this is 22, that was my rocket. I'll tell you about that later. It came from our ship." Later I remember buying a number of beers at the bar for that one.

Soc Trang, Vietnam
July 6, 1968

Dear Mom, Dad, & Family,

We are pretty busy lately what with our normal flying program and doing some writing for news releases and doing work on the company newspaper. I have not started counting the days yet and still haven't decided yet for sure on R & R. Everything here is as well as could be expected and am still learning more and more each day in the way of gun tactics. I appreciate your frequent letters and hope that all are in good health. I will write again soon. Perhaps then I will have something to say. I'm pretty tied up tonight and not much comes to mind. You are all often in my thoughts.

Love,
Your Son, Fred

We had regular opportunities to practice emergency procedures while flying combat missions in Vietnam. Crew chiefs started a tradition when they had ridden through a tail rotor failure in a Huey that they later expanded to encompass surviving engine failures and autorotations as well. The tail rotor chain drive on a Huey was particularly vulnerable to failure because its gearbox was filled with oil. I believe this was corrected in later models of the Huey by having it encased in grease, but in the B and D models we flew, if you took a round in the tail rotor gearbox and

This is what a Lycoming T53-L-11 turbine engine looks like with the inspection panels removed. It had 1,100 shaft horsepower. Empty weight was 4,500 pounds and gross weight was 8,500 pounds. The fuel tank held 206 gallons, and it burned about 68 gallons per hour. It had an endurance of about three hours or a range of about 300 miles. These panels were neither armored nor bulletproof, so the engine became a prime target of the enemy. The engine burned JP-4 jet fuel, and sometimes we "hot fueled" them and rearmed them with rockets and ammunition with the engine running so we could turn them around on missions and be back on station when troops were in contact and in need of assistance. Our engines were operating in a hostile environment right at or over gross weight and often near exhaust gas temperature red line when fully armed on many missions. With the humid hot weather of Vietnam, we often had to scrape the skids off the runway with sparks flying to get them into forward flight and into translational lift. They were generally very reliable engines, and we pushed them to their limits.

the oil drained out, the drive chain could break, and you were in for an exciting ride. A helicopter without a tail rotor can fly forward flight but requires a very skilled pilot and artful control touch initiating a running landing to even hope of salvaging the situation. If it occurs at a hover, the aircraft fuselage will start rotating and accelerating in the opposite direction than the rotor is turning and requires immediate action, called a hovering autorotation. We practiced both of these in our flight training. When a crew survived a tail rotor failure or an engine failure, the crew chief salvaged a tail rotor chain from the junk pile and made it into a bracelet.

Soc Trang, Vietnam
July 18, 1968

Dear Mom, Dad, and Family,

The berets and black T shirts are part of our uniform in the gun platoon though I prefer wearing the surfer shirt & cut offs on my down days. In the cockpit I'm holding the flex site with which I fire the 4 machine guns. Each ship has 2 rocket pods of 7 each & flexible mounted machine guns. Inside we have grenades for marking and a few hand weapons in case we're brought down. The Vikings is our name and we're known throughout the IV Corps Delta area. Things got a little hot a few weeks ago when we had two ships shot down but now they are cooling off, we hope. I have six months down, six months to go—750 hours of combat flight time. I am really looking forward to R and R and of course Christmas and getting home. Trying to do my best, miss you all very much.

Love,
Your Son, Fred

12

Kick the Tire,
Light the Fire, and Go

The mission board in flight operations looked very different and a little ominous on this day. The destination for a Viking light fire team and a Tiger Agent Orange spray ship was a place called Duong Dong airstrip on Phu Quoc island off the west coast of Vietnam up near the Cambodian border. The point of departure from the Vietnam coast would be near a cement plant north of the town of Rach Gia and south of the seaport town of Ha Tien. I had had previous missions to these areas at the far reaches of the west end of the country that involved resupplying the Special Forces camps on the western coast and along the Cambodian border in the Seven Mountains area.

Ha Tien was a vibrant seaport town with people fishing an inner harbor area. It included a downtown of shops and storefronts, and was famous for jewelry and decorations made out of tortoise shells and restaurants with seafood specialties. The Special Forces unit was located in an old, quirky, multi-leveled villa up on a promontory overlooking the harbor and the town. I admired the courage of the few advisors who lived and worked there because they seemed to have a closer and more thorough knowledge and relationship with their Vietnamese counterparts. This probably was because of the nature of their being reliant on the locals for their own security and livelihood. If I had another life to live, I would have liked to have also been a Green Beret. The training for this elite group of Army advisors involved a special background in the history and language of the indigenous people as well as being special weapons, survival, and paratrooper qualified.

Rach Gia was right on the edge of a huge former Michelin tire rubber plantation and northern parts of the triple canopy U–Minh forest. One got a foreboding feeling flying into its remote dirt airstrip, a place where you sensed a predominantly Viet Cong presence that could manifest itself at the drop of a hat. Usually, there was no action right at the airport, but occasionally you got plinked at on approach in a lightly armed slick transport. Rarely did they fire at a gunship for fear of releasing the firepower within. Occasionally, on ash-and-trash missions there, I would enjoy watching the Air America (CIA) pilots landing in a turbine powered Dornier or Helio Courier. They wore khakis or civilian tropical clothes and looked like they stepped out of a Humphrey Bogart and Katharine Hepburn movie like *The African Queen.* I wondered what secret missions they were on as they seamlessly slipped in and out of the dirt airstrip.

The cement plant in between these two places along the coast seemed out of place and time. It produced much of the cement used in the urban areas and temples of Vietnam and had a modern feel and look in an otherwise agrarian and fishing village type of area. This whole section of Vietnam seemed out of character and a strange mix of the old and the new.

Phuc Quoc island had a bay to the west that was deep enough that it was used for anchoring and for refueling large Navy ships. An unseen but important piece of infrastructure was a beacon system for vectoring B-52s from Thailand via the Bay of Kompong Som into Vietnam. Here they engaged in carpet-bombing missions with iconic names like "Rolling Thunder." Phuc Quoc also had a well-kept secret that we would be shown. There were "tiger cages," prison cells dug into the sand and dirt and topped with bamboo prison bars that held both North Vietnamese and Viet Cong prisoners of war. How they got out to this remote site I never found out, but there were quite a few of them, and we would be asked to add something to the fear factor and threat of dire consequences for attempting to escape for the enemy prisoners.

To reach Phuc Quoc we flew from Soc Trang to the cement plant as a formation flight and then took a westerly heading for the island.

There was a point in the flight when we could see neither the island nor the mainland behind us. After some time, feeling just a little uncomfortable with this experience in "no man's land over water," our destination came into view. The runway at Dong Duong was on the northern tip of the island and ran from east to west from one shore to the other. We descended and came in over the water to land on the island's airstrip. There were a few thatched-roof houses adjacent to the runway. A couple of jeeps met us and took us to a small base a short distance away, where on a white sand beach there was a club-type structure for the Navy personnel assigned there. On the beach they had a ski boat, surfboards, and inflatable rafts. It was like arriving on the TV set of *Fantasy Island.* What kind of a war are these guys fighting?

Compared to old Soc Trang's revetments, sandbagged hooches, and even the Tigers' Den, it felt like we had landed in paradise. The first night, we had great food and lots of beer and went swimming in the sea. One crewmember fell asleep in a rubber raft and drifted out about 100 yards, and we all yelled to wake him up and then laughed as we watched him paddling aggressively back towards the shore.

We slept in some austere quarters there, and the next day we started our assigned mission, which was to spray Agent Orange on a road from the Tiger UH-1D spray ship "Beer, Bullets and Blood," while our light fire team of two gunships flew behind and below to provide gun cover. The road ran generally through the island lengthwise, and the whole landscape felt like a scene from a *M*A*S*H* television episode, where a few isolated "machine gun charlies" were more of a nuisance than a threat. We sprayed the entire road over about three or four days of flying defoliation missions while enjoying the beach and the island scenery at the end of each day. We had little contact with the enemy except for a handful of incidents. I believe our goal was to make the road safer for the sailors assigned there to drive from one end of the island to the other by stripping away the ground cover. As the mission was winding down, one of the officers with some sort of responsibility for the POW camp asked if we would fly the gunships over the top of the "tiger cages" and fire the mini guns over the top of them to remind the prisoners not to try to escape. We obliged the request, and I still remember looking down into those cages dug into the island sand with their bamboo bars and the prisoners in them.

As the mission was completed, the crew chief let me know that he was concerned about play in the trunnion bearing on the overhead rotor system of our B model gunship. I wondered whether the play had become so excessive that we might have to stay there longer since this was more like a trip to Vung Tau for in-country R&R than a combat assault mission. But in the end I realized that we trusted our lives to that bearing and that he knew the acceptable tolerances and had consulted the other crew chiefs as well. Regardless, the rotor system was compromised and the aircraft needed to be sling loaded off the island, and my crew and I rode in the back of the Innkeepers Chinook while the other gunship and spray ship made the trip back to Soc Trang. While we were en route, the pilot of the Chinook said over the intercom, "You guys are pretty brave coming out here in those single-engine Hueys. These are some of the most shark-infested waters in all of Vietnam." That comment got our attention.

Soc Trang, Vietnam
July 22, 1968

Dear Mom, Dad, and Family,

... All in all I received about $60 from the Seminary ... went a long way in purchasing supplies, clothing, and medical aid for the children in the orphanage in downtown Soc Trang. The checks presented a small problem as there are no facilities on post that will cash personal two-party checks. In town they just deal in piasters and have no concept of bank or check accounts, so you see it would be impossible to do something like sign a check over to them. So I worked things out with a captain here who had a checking account. I signed the checks over to him and he purchased the items with me. I'm going to check with the orphanage and see what they need, then I'll tell you what the deal is, and maybe we can work out a joint effort to help them out a little. We so appreciate everyone's interest. So just wait a short while and I'll check it out. The sisters are very dedicated and do a real fine job in the face of many obstacles.

I now write up all of the proposed Awards and Decorations for our platoon as well as the company newspaper and the normal flying schedule. It all keeps me pretty busy … 90 degrees out and the sun is very hot. It will rain around 2 o'clock like always…. We have had the chance to help a lot of ground troops out of some tight jams lately We

This is a typical picture of a Vietnamese hooch in a rural area. This would probably be the home of a Vietnamese farmer and his family. Or it could be a place for hiding mortars and Vietcong weapons and ammunition. The problem is you don't know exactly what this is. If you found this hooch in the middle of a landing zone where the week previous a lot of enemy contact had been part of landing here, then you would probably first fly down a tree line and over the area in a gunship and see of you could draw fire. If you did draw fire, you would probably return fire and see if it escalated. If it did escalate from single shots to automatic and semi-automatic weapons, then you would return fire, and if it was coming from these hooches, you would probably roll in with a few rockets and increase your altitude off the top of the trees because a rocket might touch off a secondary explosion if in fact there were arms and ammunition stored in the hooch. So there ends up being few situations where you can just assume that what you see is what you are going to get.

have also been blowing up our share of VC huts and bunkers and getting them in the open once and a while for some confirmed kills.

Love, Your Son Fred

The front-end view of this B model Huey gunship may not have any significance to the casual viewer, but deeper inspection reveals a story that has personal meaning for me. The windshield on the left has a white border indicating it was recently replaced and, in all likelihood, shot out on a recent mission. I cannot claim any personal war story for that one. But the chin bubbles, the lower pieces of plexiglass, both also have white borders around them, and I am responsible for at least one of those being replaced.

We were flying a mission somewhere north of Binh Thuy Air Base, where the Ninth Infantry Division was operating after a concentrated B-52 carpet-bombing mission with a light gun team of two gunships. The area was completely obliterated from the intense bombing and unrecognizable in terms of relating to our position on the tactical map. I was the aircraft commander in the lead gunship. We were low-leveling and wondering where the hell we were without ground references from the bombing. The place sort of looked like a moonscape.

While monitoring the artillery frequency, we heard announced, "Artillery going into RP4." We then confirmed that our location was too near RP4 on the map as an explosion occurred about 50 meters in front of us. I turned sharply at treetop level to get away, and the top of a lone surviving tree popped up right in front of our flight path and whacked out the chin bubble, leaving the remnants of the top of the tree sticking half in and half out, an embarrassing but at least not fatal occurrence. Once again, we had dodged a bullet. Maintenance seemed quite interested in hearing the backstory of this mission, and I think we speculated that there might have been a mine placed high in a tree on our pass. At any rate, the chin bubble probably needed replacing anyway as all of our ships were tacked together and old, but I'm sure it went on to fly many more missions.

Soc Trang, Vietnam
July 29, 1968

Dear Mom, Dad, and Family,

I just got back from an unusual assignment. With a two-ship fire team we escorted two ships out to Duong Dong Island off the western coast near the border of South Vietnam and Cambodia. We couldn't believe our eyes when we landed. The Air Force and Navy have small bases there (they always seem to catch the good places). There were white sand beaches, blue lagoons, and a surf with about five foot waves. The VC were isolated in the middle mountainous tree-lined areas so the rest of the island was relatively secure. We escorted and covered the slick as they sprayed defoliation spray on an overgrown road, which ran the length of the Island. Not much trouble … a little fire in the mountain passes etc. but nothing that we couldn't handle. And were able to spend a few hours between runs soaking up the sun on this tropical beach paradise. It was a real exhilarating experience after seven months of nothing but flat rice paddies and mud. Well now we're back and we wouldn't believe that there actually was such an island if it weren't for the sunburn and sand in all of our clothes. It was a real welcome break.

I am working with a captain to get some help for a Vietnamese hospital downtown. We got the orphanage pretty well squared away with the generous donations from the Seminarians and church groups many officers knew. We are raising cain with the VC. I'm in great health, and glad to hear from you so frequently.

Love,
Your Son, Fred

This was the control tower for our airfield. In many respects this control tower was the best seat in the house for observing the surrounding area and rice paddies. When mortars were fired at our airfield, as they were frequently during 1968, they were usually heard first as distinctive whoomps but first seen in the control tower as muzzle flashes. The tower would then turn on a siren, and everyone on the airfield except for the gunship pilots would head for the sandbagged bunkers that were distributed around the airfield. The gunships would scramble, roll in on the flashes and tubes and expend their ordnance, the mortaring would stop, and the all-clear signal would be given by the tower and everyone would come out and survey the damage and then begin reporting in through the chain of command where the damage occurred. There were times when hooches were hit and people were injured. The post office was hit once and some of the mail destroyed. There was damage done to helicopters and support vehicles. There were occasionally lives lost during these attacks. They were a very scary enemy attack on our airfield.

* * *

Our gunships were usually "combat cocked." That meant that we had gone through what was normally a fairly lengthy checklist of preflight items down to the last two steps and left the helicopter at the ready for immediate starting under combat conditions. When we were on standby we never knew when the horn would sound for a mission. In addition to responding to mortar attacks on our own airfield, we were scrambled when we had an aircraft down, when troops were in contact and in danger of being outgunned, or when an infantry soldier was injured, and their unit needed an immediate medevac. We also got called to unsecured areas when a Dust-off helicopter needed gun cover or for any one of a number of requests that came in to our operations office regularly for immediate support due to an unfolding combat situation. Every crewmember knew what needed to be done in a scramble, and they inevitably responded to the horn by running out to the flight line and readying the aircraft for immediate takeoff. Crewmembers need to put on flak jackets and helmets themselves, pull the bulletproof panels forward on the sides of the pilots, close the pilot doors and secure them, and strap themselves into their position for takeoff as the engine spooled up to operating RPM. Then the intercom came alive with a staccato set of internal and external questions and responses—"21, 22 is ready"—and then internal questions and responses—"crew ready, ready up, coming up, clear left, on the go."

And then the call to the tower from lead: "Soc Trang Tower, Flight of Two Vikings, on the go, departing revetments to north on runway 36 and a west departure from the crosswind." The crew chief and door gunner picked up their M 60s, laid them across their laps, and settled into their positions at the ready for returning fire sitting on the web seats in the back.

Soc Trang, Vietnam
August 10, 1968

Dear Mom, Dad, and Family,

… After the last 7-½ months I feel like I am 42 not almost 22. The people here are very bad off.

Of course you couldn't tell it by the way they laugh and have such sincere yet simple dispositions.

For not even having a potato sack to wear I think they have a few secrets to real happiness, that we in all of our riches are often too blind to see. I don't agree with the idea that what they don't know they won't miss for everyone is entitled to at least clothes and medical supplies. When I have so much…. I feel a little guilty. I guess it will seem remote and far out of reach when I get home but seeing these people every day the need is very intense.

I was flying wingman today off another ship in the lead. On the main control cyclic stick there are a number of buttons grouped close together among them a stabilization system and the firing button for the rockets. On the deck we fly with the stabilization

This is a picture of the open-air market area in downtown Soc Trang. There are flowers, fruits and vegetables, fish and meats, and live animals, and it is the center of commerce for a Vietnamese city like Soc Trang. There are shops selling all sorts of American-related items on the black market. The usual currency was piasters, but most shops would also deal in military pay. There were artisan shops that did fine art and paintings and all types of services, restaurants, and motor vehicle and scooter repair shops, etc. The military currency that was used throughout Vietnam was changed randomly to inhibit the black market, causing distress among the merchants who dealt in this area and found the currency overnight to be worthless.

system set so that if one pilot gets hit the aircraft will climb up instead of dive into the ground. Well we just let down and you guessed it I went to set the stabilization system and punched off a rocket, and it blew up right under the lead aircraft. I lost a few years of life in a second because I thought for sure that I'd shot down the lead gunship. Well we carried on and had a pretty good day, zapped about 5 VC we caught in the open in black uniforms, and the ground troops we covered got a lot of confirmed kills also.

Love, Your son, Fred

13

The Magic Carpet Ride

October 18, 1968, is a date I will remember for the rest of my life. We were assigned a mission to the U-Minh Forest with a light gun team in an attempt to locate an officer who had been a prisoner of war and at the time had been held in captivity for about four years.

We left Soc Trang at about 3:00 in the morning as a flight of two heavily armed gunships and were en route to Camau in the southern part of the IV Corps area of Vietnam. These missions always evoked a heightened level of anticipation because the areas outside of Camau were notorious bad guy territory consisting of multiple canals, defunct rubber plantations, triple canopy jungle, and lots of opportunity for Viet Cong to exist in the relative protection of their natural surroundings.

We climbed to 1,500 feet, an altitude that was high for a gun team that usually flies its combat missions at treetop level. At that altitude, the temperature was a bit cooler. Our light fire team was flying along smoothly in the night air. It was a very dark night and raining, and the upcoming mission was on everybody's mind. The radio was tuned to Paddy Control, but there was little traffic in the early morning hours of an otherwise quiet day. The old B model was humming along, and the gauges were in the green.

About a half hour into the flight, we were about 30 miles out of Soc Trang at about 95 knots when the RPM gauge started jumping up and down slightly. As I scanned the instrument panel, I noticed the exhaust gas temperature gauge was going off the top end, telling me that the engine was probably ingesting itself. Other gauges were flickering, and the RPM started dropping. We had been trained over and over about the importance of taking decisive action when the engine fails. You don't really have time to debate alternative actions in a single-engine helicopter with an engine failure. The helicopter is designed so that, in the event of an engine failure, you lower the collective control. This disconnects the engine from the rotor blades like a clutch on a motorcycle, and the blades keep spinning with the weight of the descending helicopter and the resultant air coming up through them.

I entered an autorotation and then went through the process of checking off emergency procedures that included shutting off the fuel flow to the engine. Now we were committed to landing somewhere down in the dark area beneath our flight path. Looking down at the black hole beneath us didn't seem like a very promising prospect, but we had no other options at that point. I made a call to Paddy Control that I had rehearsed in my mind for such a time: "Mayday, mayday, mayday, this is Viking 23 with an engine failure approximately 30 klicks out of Soc Trang en route to Camau in the Delta."

The controller on the other end amped up the pitch in his voice and said there was a Dustoff medevac helicopter in the area that would be en route. It felt like he was pulling for us.

I responded, "Roger that!"

I proceeded with the shutdown and securing of systems in the aircraft and found the cockpit so black that I turned the master back on to include the instrument lights so I could see the airspeed and mentally noted the altitude going through 1,000. I thought I would need the landing light to see where we were touching down. Our wingman was following us down. At 300 feet, I turned on the landing light, and to my surprise there was a muddy field right in front of us. I flared the aircraft at about 50 and then pulled the final pitch back into the blades at about five. We sank into the muddy rice paddy. The aircraft started to pitch forward, but the mud was thick enough that it held us from rolling over forward and it settled back down into the muck. Whew! We had made it.

I yelled for the crew to pull the guns off the ship and set up a perimeter while we waited for Dustoff. We could see from some tracers that our wingman was taking some fire from a tree line to the west, and returning some as well, as he set up a wide circular pattern around our downed aircraft in the open rice paddy. The medevac was on approach in about 10 minutes and on the ground at the rear of our downed aircraft in about five more minutes. We loaded our weapons and flight gear in the D model Huey with the welcome red cross on the doors, and the four of us climbed in and exited the area. Sometime shortly afterwards, the wingman observed the aircraft explode, either from a bullet or charge, and we never saw it again.

The Dustoff helicopter returned us to Soc Trang. I remember going before the operations officer for a debriefing. He wanted to know all of the details, what readings we had on the instruments, what actions we took, and how the crew performed, etc. That part was somewhat of a blur because I was sort of hyped up on adrenaline by then. The next thing I remember was being in the Tigers' Den having a can of chili for breakfast, feeling excited about the incident, happy for the successful autorotation and the extraction of our crew, and thankful for the luck of a muddy rice paddy opening up in our flight path. Later, upon reflection, it sank in and felt like we had really lucked out this time.

In 2015, my wife Shannon and I attended a reunion of the 121st Aviation Association in Fort Worth, Texas. These are attended by pilots and flight crewmembers and their spouses and family members. I walked up to a group of crew chiefs and door gunners at the bar and asked, "Do any of you remember going through a night engine failure in October of 1968 in a Viking gunship?"

One good old boy from Tennessee said, "I was on that ship. I've been telling my family about that adventure all my life."

I said, "I was the aircraft commander."

It turns out that Paul Woodby was the door gunner on that memorable ride. He went on after Vietnam to run a string of bail bond companies in Tennessee. He later borrowed from the popular Steppenwolf song of the 1960s the phrase "magic carpet ride" to describe our shared experience. We particularly enjoyed each other's company at that reunion and have been friends on social media ever since. We have a bond from that shared experience that transcends the years. We have exchanged memorabilia over the years, but the memory of that experience was a defining one for both of us and will be with us for the rest of our lives.

> **Soc Trang, Vietnam**
> Wednesday, August 14, 1968

Dear Mom, Dad, and Family,

Not much new in the way of the war here. It's raining quite a bit. Last night I was on firefly and had to come down three times because the weather got too bad. Most of the rice paddies of the Delta are submerged and all you can see around Soc Trang is miles and miles of water with trees and towns occasionally.

> Love,
> Your Son, Fred

> Soc Trang, Vietnam
> Thursday, August 15, 1968

Dear Nana,

Well hello from the wonderful Far East Paradise of Soc Trang, Vietnam.

Not much new. It rains like all get out lately as we are in the middle of the monsoon season. My roommate just got back from R and R in Bangkok and came back with some very fine silks and bronze ware so am debating whether to go there. I think will go on R and R at the end of November. It's a long way off.

… I was out tooling around in the operational area at 90 miles per hour about 10' above the ground turned and a tree grew right up in front of my flight path. Well the only tree in the area and I hit the top of it. The tree knocked out the plastic chin bubble below my feet and but for a good scare we came out all the better for wear. It got a little windy in the cockpit as we flew the only "air conditioned" B model around in a rain storm.

A lot of this place depends on your attitude and I am fortunate with a number of very good friends Thanks again for writing so often and hello to all the relatives down Tacoma way.

Love,
Your grandson, Fred

Soc Trang, Vietnam
Monday, August 26, 1968

Dear Nan, Aunt B, Uncle J, and Relatives,

… A few nights ago the VC decided to lob a few mortar rounds in on us. As you recall when I flew transports I could hit the floor or make it for the bunker. In guns it's a little different. We have to run out to the line and get the gunships airborne as they are our first line of defense. Then we form up in our respective fire teams and put rocket attacks in on the mortar positions. Usually as soon as we get airborne they stop lest we make waste of their positions but charging out through the barrage to get the ships cranked and airborne is quite an experience. Everything in you says "stay on the floor"

Large woven baskets were the primary means of transporting farm goods or handmade items to the market along with sampan boats that brought goods to Soc Trang via the canals that connected with the Song Hau River. The women were the primary transporters of agricultural goods and could be seen along roads and paths leading into the city either carrying large baskets on poles across their shoulders or individual baskets balanced on their heads. When they arrived at the market, they could be seen resting by squatting down and balancing their bodies in a resting position while they sold their wares in the market. In contrast there were also professional women dressed in áo dàis who worked in businesses, hotels, and financial institutions in Soc Trang.

This is operations or flight ops. The two symbols on either side of the entrance remind you that everything here is a team effort. The growling Tiger with bared teeth and the lightning bolt is on one side of the entrance. The Viking with his arms loaded down with 2.75 rockets is on the other. Through this opening you will walk to find out what your mission will be for the day. This is where the days begin and, when you return from 10 to 14 hours in the cockpit, this is where they end, and you turn in your aircraft daily flight records. Some people walk in these doors in the morning and are not here in the evening to check out. Will today be your day for the thrill of victory or the agony of defeat? What adventures do the mission board hold for you and your crew today?

but next thing you know you are making it to the flight line and it's quite a relief to get in the air. It's a little different pace from the old silent walls of the Seminary, huh? Well I really eat this stuff up but it scares the living daylights out of me once in a while.

The rains came yesterday. Talk about the N.W. It rained 4.5" here yesterday. That's in one day! We'll all need web feet pretty soon.

Yesterday also we worked up around the 7 Mountains Region. You might ask your friend about her brother as it is near the Cambodian border. We often work with Special Forces units all along the border in IV corps maybe he is at one of the outposts I used to resupply in transports.

Sincerely, Cousin Fred

Soc Trang, Vietnam
Wednesday, August 28, 1968

Dear Mom, Dad, and Family,

...a couple of hours before I go up again tonight. This week our fire team has airport security. I'm training another pilot in the tactics of flying the wing ship and there is word in the breeze of me being one of the three fire team leaders in the Company. It would mean being the aircraft commander in the lead aircraft and making the decisions for the fire team as well as instructions given to the transports on airmobile assaults. It is quite a responsibility like knowing where all the friendlies are in a large operation for you carry quite a bit of firepower with you … it is the highest position of control and responsibility that a warrant officer can attain. In fact right now the only fire team leaders in the company are a Captain, a Chief Warrant Officer, and a First Lieutenant. Well we'll just have to see. Right now I am "Viking 22" maybe by the next time I write I'll be "23." It is something to try for at any rate. Enough war stories!

I got your first package of baby clothing etc. For future reference on such things as sweaters are very cute but it stays around 90 degrees here year round and with the very high humidity light clothing is most desirable I just broke 1,000 hours of combat flight time the other day. I am getting to know the IV Corps area like my backyard, I don't think I will ever regret this year.

Love,
Your Son, Fred

14

Lead Gunship Goes Down

We were flying wing in a Viking light gun team. We had been requested to join an operation with troops in contact in an area north of Soc Trang, and we were entering into the operational area. I was the pilot and Steve Richards, a first lieutenant, was the aircraft commander. As we entered the operation area, our lead took fire and reported breaking to the right. The aircraft began a turn and just kept rolling and impacted the ground and rolled over about four times. Miraculously the ship did not catch fire. It all happened so fast that it felt like the picture we were seeing was in slow motion. The crew chief was thrown out of the aircraft on impact, and the ship rolled over on him, taking his life.

Steve didn't hesitate but said immediately to me, "Mac, hold on, we are going down there and getting them. You see that tree line where the enemy fire is coming and the dike line in between the downed aircraft and the tree line? That is where we are going to land."

I said, "Roger that."

As we descended, he added, "You and the crew start firing when we are on approach and don't quit." He spotted a place on the dike and began the approach. I started firing into the tree line and subconsciously felt my body scrunch down a little lower in my seat behind my bullet bouncer and kept firing short bursts into the tree line while the door gunner and crew chief also added their machine gun fire.

We were laying down suppressive fire to get their attention off the downed bird. Bullet casings were bouncing around the inside of the helicopter and the noise was deafening. It felt like we were one hell of a sitting duck on that dike. Steve didn't hesitate for a minute. I thought, "Man, this guy has got ice water in his veins."

He said over the intercom, "We are staying here until the crew is on board." We didn't know at the time that the crew chief had been killed in the rollover. His name was Specialist George S. Hudzinga.

The two pilots and the door gunner got out of the destroyed B model and moved across the rice paddy and threw themselves, totally

covered with mud and out of breath, into the back end of our aircraft.
We noticed there were only three of them. One of them yelled that the
crew chief didn't make it. And something like, "Let's get the hell out of
here."

We were taking fire from the tree line and it was not a place to linger.
Steve pulled pitch and pedal turned the aircraft so the ass-end was pointed
toward the hot tree line, and in a few seconds we were racing across the rice
paddy and climbing out of the area. A report determined that the aircraft
had taken fire in the engine area. As a company, we all felt the loss of Specialist George Hudzinga. It was a reminder of the risks that we faced each
day on these missions.

The sights, sounds, smells and experiences along the flight line of Soc Trang Airfield remind you that you are not in Kansas anymore. The banana trees bend in
the hot blast furnace of the dry season in the Mekong Delta. There are snakes
that come out of the rice paddies at night. If you leave the light on in your room
at night while you are throwing them down in the Tigers' Den, you return to the
light being covered with black bugs. A rat darts across the floor in the mess hall
and you focus on the food you are eating and don't dwell on the apparition. You
jump when the outgoing artillery fires off without a warning. The generators
keeping the lights on grind out their ever-present tune. The smell of JP-4 jet fuel
fills your nostrils. The siren goes off and you find yourself in a dank, dark bunker with 20 other men half joking half wondering if this time the mortar men
are going to get lucky and hit your bunker. Of all the places you could be at 21
years old, how the hell did you end up here?

Soc Trang, Vietnam
Thursday, September 5, 1968

Dear Mom, Dad, and Family,

I have decided to wait until about two weeks before I am scheduled to return stateside before going on R and R.

From many experiences here, getting the clothes and money for the Vietnamese, and from my talks with the local chaplain I have thought a lot lately about the brotherhood or a similar life. If I could find one that needed a gunship driver I'd be set. In all seriousness I am trying to consider what I will be in the future as there is much time for contemplating what you want to do in your life.

We have received two of the clothing packages so far. I hear it is raining a little at home. Well in that case I will be well prepared to return to the Northwest as all it does here is rain. The situation here remains moderate and no room for complaint but it gets a little tense once in a while.

Thank you very much Mom & Dad for both of your recent letters they were indeed well read and anxiously awaited. I am in fine health and everything is going well. I hope you at home are doing as well and in equally good health. So long for now you are often in my thoughts.

Love
Your Son
Fred

Soc Trang, Vietnam
Friday, September 6, 1968

Dear Mom, Dad, and Family,

Well I finally made it. I flew fire team lead today. There were a few rough edges but nothing that a little experience won't fix up. I worked with transport flights of from 10 to 18 aircraft putting troops in on combat assaults in about 8 different landing zones around a major canal junction objective area. The weather gave us a little problem and we got zapped at a few times but the lifts came off well and none of the aircraft took any hits, so apparently, we were successful in providing good cover and fire on the assaults. The officers in the command and control ship remarked that it was a real fine day. It was a feeling that is quite hard to express to be controlling and covering all those assets. It was sort of a rewarding highpoint after the many hours of training and preparation to take over the position....

Well just wanted to share a very rewarding experience with you. I could never have had the experience or one of equal satisfaction had it not been for this tour. I feel a little strange. Everyone says too bad you have to go to Vietnam and all but I wouldn't trade this year for any other experience wise. Don't get me wrong though, I can't wait to get home.

Everything is going well, think of you often. Love,

Your Son, Fred

* * *

I have hugged the deck, flat out at 85 knots over the tree lines and avoided the open rice paddies of the Mekong Delta. Down, down, down

This heavy fire team—three Viking gunships—is returning from a successful mission with smoke grenades popped on the skids, flying in formation, and celebrating the way fighter pilots have done since the beginning of combat aviation. Everyone on Soc Trang Airfield felt the thrill of victory when an occasional flyby like this occurred.

we went below the treetops dodging ominous canal intersections and mud-filled bomb craters weaving back and forth making it hard to lead us with a strategic shot.

I have popped a tree line and had a Viet Cong in black pajamas empty an AK-47 in my face and miss! I have heard the hammers of hell pounding on the fuselage with rounds piercing the thin sheet metal. I have felt the ominous presence of eyes and guns ready to open fire northwest of Camau, in the plantations adjoining the U-Minh Forest, while looking for a POW camp and a captured Green Beret major.

I have lost friends who were there one day and gone the next ... without being able to understand how or why. I have heard the rumors of grenades in the gas tank with a rubber band around them and the pin pulled, waiting for the fuel to eat away at the rubber and obliterate a Huey and its crew when least expected. I thought about these rumors each time I pre-flighted and looked in the fuel tank with a flashlight and knew I couldn't see the far reaches in the corner inside the tank.

I have reloaded the tubes with 2.75 rockets, saying a prayer the first few times I placed the rocket body on my knee and cranked the warhead on with one solid jerk. I have pushed the nose over and pounded the target dodging tracers, knowing I was seeing only a few of the rounds in the tracers coming at us, and held the nose down until the runs were made, the target was hit, and all 14 rockets were away.

I learned to keep a calm, low-pitched voice calling "mayday, mayday, mayday" when the engine failed at 2,000 feet one night, in a fully loaded B model gunship and we autorotated in … and I said a silent "thank you" when I turned on the landing light at 300 feet and there was a muddy clearing in front of me. I have pulled pitch just right, that one time you get … and then we slammed into the oozing mud while the tracers were shot at us by some unknown VC from a tree line to the west.

I have heard the unforgettable call sign "Dustoff inbound on short final," and been swept up and away and out of the mud and the dark and the fear. I have felt the loss of a ship as the VC blew her up before daylight. I was back home in the Tigers' Den having a can of chili at the bar for breakfast. We never saw her again.

I have slept in my boots with a loaded .45 under my pillow and my jungle fatigues around my ankles when I first was in-country. I was ready for whatever, at the distinct sound of the incoming mortars leaving the tubes on their way to the target, and the airfield siren signaling their impending arrival.

I have agonized many times as the turbine spooled up ever so slowly on a scramble as a gunship aircraft commander while the Viet Cong walked the mortars down the flight line towards us, blowing the hell out of the runway and some of the aircraft.

I have flown the "midnight special" … gun cover for a Dustoff medevacing wounded from Seven Canals, low level, circling, lights out, pitch black, silence, sweat, and head on a swivel … with a couple of weeks left in my tour.

And I have reached out for the hand of God and made promises to him, asking him to pull me out of these adventures … and to me it felt like he did … time after time.

I did this. I was scared to death a lot of the time; but I did this for 1,300 hours of combat missions in one year.

I was a Vietnam helicopter pilot. I was a Blue Tiger slick pilot then aircraft commander with the Tigers and a gunship pilot and aircraft commander at 21 years old, call sign Viking 23 of the Blue Diamond Devils of the Delta, with the 121st Assault Helicopter Company based at Soc Trang, RVN. I was a Soc Trang Tiger for the first half of my tour and a Viking for the second half. We were 100 miles south of Saigon at an airfield surrounded by rice paddies in the Mekong Delta of South Vietnam during 1967–1968 and the experiences changed my life … forever.

Soc Trang, Vietnam
Friday, September 13, 1968

Dear Mom, Dad, and Family,

... So far I have received three bundles of clothing and powders etc. and today I ventured downtown to the orphanage ... the nuns were there. I met Sister Mary Martha the Mother Superior of the orphanage/school. The grounds themselves are very gracious in comparison to the humble surroundings of Soc Trang City. The orphanage/school complex itself was constructed in 1951 by the French and is cement of structure and two stories high, in a rather traditional Vietnamese-French design with high ceilings and archway corridors but without windows or doors. In one wing the Sisters of Providence run a day school for local Catholic children. The orphans ranging from a few days old to about 10. The most touching sight was an entire room of mal-formed and premature babies. Sister Martha introduced me to the nun and the women volunteers in this section and remarked at the fine job that these women do. Sister said almost one baby dies every day, the job is a very demanding one. If a child can live for a few months at least then there is a good chance for the child. I noticed in particular a child with hands so small they would fit inside my ring without the energy to brush the many flies from around his face. For a moment I stopped by their chapel as the nuns were chanting the litany. It was a very rewarding touch of reality in this war torn and confused country.

Love,
Your Son, Fred

Soc Trang, Vietnam
Saturday, September 21, 1968

Dear Mom, Dad, and Family,

Well thank you very much for the many funny cards and newsy letters of late. I have had quite a few interesting missions lately and it seems like the more you learn some new aspect opens up and you realize how much more there is to know. I am taking over as "Viking 23" fire team leader and my long-time friend, Jim Lucking, from way back at preflight is team leader of the "21" fire team. We alternate as primary mission team every other day or so and the platoon leader whose job is concerned with mostly running the platoon also flies lead when he gets the time. Have 1,100 combat hours to date. I am looking forward to a package or so as I only received three of the ones you sent. The captain I worked with on the orphanage and hospital returned home so I was designated the Civic Affairs Officer and now I am awaiting the developing of some pictures so I can send out some letters and give the program a good kick in the rear. As Awards and Decorations Officer for the platoon I'm finally getting everyone written up. ... Well I am busy and time is flying by. I hope you are all in good spirits.

You are often in my thoughts. Everything is fine.

Love,
Your Son, Fred

Soc Trang, Vietnam
Sunday, October 6, 1968

Dear Mom, Dad, and Family,

Well thanks for all of the cards on my birthday.... The winds are shifting.

This is a signal of the transition period between the wet season and the beginning of the dry. Now we are experiencing some quite severe thunderstorms which add a real challenge to our job. In between the sun is very hot, and it feels good to lie out and soak up the rays when we have time. All of a sudden the old people are gone home and now we are the ones teaching the new people what we have learned by word of mouth and trial and error. In the next A & D ceremony I am getting the Air Medal with V Device for Valor when our wing man got shot down and we landed to pick up the three surviving crew members. It was a pretty hot area and so they wrote us up for the action. We have a new platoon leader, a new Major with no previous gunship time and what with our now having so many new pilots the other fire team lead and I will have our hands full pulling our regular missions as well as a rigid training schedule for the younger pilots and the new Major.

We have had a little activity around the airfield lately with Charlie and the local VC mortar men. This week I'm up again as a counter-mortar force and a first line of air defense should the airfield be hit. I think if I could get transitioned into the Huey Cobra I would extend for a while but that's highly unlikely.... I'm a fire team leader and it's really a rewarding job to help out the ground troops.

Love,
Your Son, Fred

Soc Trang, Vietnam
Monday, October 8, 1968

Dear Mom, Dad, and Family,

Just got back from visiting my old pal Sister Mary Martha down at the Orphanage. I got together with the mess sergeant and we took them a deuce and a half load of food, the remainder of the five bundles of clothing and the medicines from Mrs. March. They were very glad to see us and most appreciative for the supplies. We have a lamb outside our hooch now, not very good as a lawnmower but a good friend. Sister gave it to us about 3 weeks ago and today she wanted to give me another so it wouldn't be lonely. Luckily I had to return for lunch before they could round me up but I'm sure we are in for another four-footed lawnmower before the month is over.

I am flying nights this week. The air is cool and unusually clear. Thunderheads form on the horizon and the fantastic lightning storms light each one up from inside like a giant Chinese lantern. It is truly a remarkable sight and one which I have seen nowhere else to such a magnificent degree.

... I am finding many more rewarding experiences every day. I think the key to a seemingly short time over here is to get involved with a few jobs and keep busy. I have had the opportunity here to do the most rewarding work I ever have before and though I fly my rear end off I still love burning up the sky.

Love,
Your Son, Fred

Soc Trang, Vietnam
Sunday, October 14, 1968

Dear Mom, Dad, and Family,

Good Morning, I hope everything is going well in school at home and at work. I got my request for an R & R approved so if everything works out I will be going on the 25th of November.

... We had a show the other day from Australia. Some singers and a modern band and an old woman something like "Phyllis Diller" type of humor and she really brought the house down.

A couple of people in our unit came down with hepatitis and infectious mono-nucleosis. We are all sore as hell from getting shots, but now the initial excitement about a potential epidemic has cooled down. I flew nights all this past week—not much action—a few outposts and patrols around the airfield ran into some trouble. We enjoyed listening to the World Series games. With the time difference they came on about 1:30am in the morning about the time you start getting sleepy and it helps to have a good program on to keep you wide awake in the air. I wonder about the presidential candidates. I realize that it is a part of campaigning to make exaggerated claims but I sure feel sorry for the people on the DMZ if they ever halt the bombing. That will be one hell of a risky tactic. If it backfires the NVA and the VC there will be so well supplied that they will really make waste of what little we have gained there.

> Love,
> Your Son,
> Fred

> Soc Trang, Vietnam
> Wednesday, October 17, 1968

Dear Nana,

Well I'm getting there. Slowly but surely the days are creeping by. I am looking forward very much to the 24th of November when I am scheduled to go to Australia for a long-awaited R & R. In the next few days I will get a 3-day pass to go to one of the more pacified seaside towns, Vung Tau, up country for a little break. I am sure glad I waited until the end to ask for any passes or R & R. This way it gives you something to look forward to and it makes the remainder of your tour seem much shorter. I still have no word on my next assignment. I am getting in a lot of flight time lately. Have close to 1,200 hours now. I hear the weather has turned cold at home and I can hardly wait to get into a cold climate for a while. Well Nana everything is about the same. I have many new experiences every day but can't wait to get home.

I just wanted to let you know I am doing real fine and in the best of spirits.

Say hello to the rest of the relatives. Think of you often.

> Love,
> Your Grandson,
> Fred

15

Bringing It All Together

John Steinbeck, recipient of both Nobel and Pulitzer prizes for his famous novels, travelled to Vietnam in 1966–67 at the request of the publisher Harry Guggenheim. He spent time in Pleiku observing and flying with the 10th Cavalry, D Troop there. Words of his describing his admiration for their skills and courage were found in personal letters published in a book *Steinbeck in Vietnam* edited by Thomas E. Barden, professor, University of Toledo.

Alicia, I wish I could tell you about these pilots. They make me sick with envy. They ride their vehicles the way a man controls a fine, well-trained quarter horse. They weave along stream beds, rise like swallows to clear trees, they turn and twist and dip like swifts in the evening. I watch their hands and feet on the controls, the delicacy of the coordination reminds me of the seeming and sure hands of [Pablo] Casals on the cello.

They are truly musicians' hands and they play their controls like music and they dance them like ballerinas and they make me jealous because I want so much to do it.

Remember your child night dreams of perfect flight free and wonderful? It's like that, and sadly I know I never can. My hands are too old and forgetful to take orders from the command center, which speaks of updrafts and sidewinds, of drift and shift, or ground fire indicated by a tiny puff or flash, or a hit and all these commands must be obeyed by the musicians' hands instantly or automatically.

I must take my longing out in admiration and the joy of seeing it.

Sorry about that leak of ecstasy, Alicia, but I had to get it out or burst.

Soc Trang, Vietnam
Tuesday, October 22, 1968

Dear Mom, Dad, and Family,

Yesterday the powers that be decided to change the military pay currency throughout Vietnam and I would imagine that this morning found many distraught Vietnamese merchants who have been profiting from the black market. We are presently in the tail end of a sizeable typhoon, which has limited our flying quite a bit for the last few days.

141

… I will be looking for a car if I get a stateside assignment and think I would just as soon get one in Seattle on leave and then drive across the states on my way to my next duty station because if it is in the states it will probably be in the South. So you might keep an eye out for about a 66 or 67 Corvette convertible. I clear about 500 a month after insurance and bonds and whatever and I will make Chief Warrant Officer in less than a month, so the upgrade in rank and pay will about equalize the loss of combat pay. I don't have any bills and think it would be a good time to get a good sports car from a financial standpoint and just to get it out of my system before I have to settle down to anything, but I don't think that will be for quite a while anyway.

I saw Sister Martha the other day and gave her your most recent package of medicine and I took some toys for the kids. They were all very happy and thankful for your generosity. Thanks again for all the letters.

Love, Your Son Fred

Soc Trang, Vietnam
Wednesday, October 23, 1968

Dear Mom, Dad, and Family,

Well just call me "Chief." I got promoted last night to Chief Warrant Officer CW2. It was indeed a happy occasion for five of us from our class of 67–19. Three of us have been flying together for two years through flight school, transports, and then gunships all hanging in there. We all had a few engine failures and managed to walk away from some pretty banged up aircraft. It's a heck of a lot of experience for 12 months. Our only regrets were that six of us came over together and as it looks only five will be coming back. A real fine guy, Ricky Hull, was killed during the Tet Offensive of this year when his ship was brought down by heavy enemy ground fire. Our class has given many to the cause and we are very proud of those who have given their lives and only wish they could share in the joy of our promotion and the anticipation we all feel at the thought of returning home.

Though at times I have had some very close calls and been scared out of my mind, in many ways I regret leaving Vietnam. I have never before felt such a feeling of accomplishment both in flying as well as my dealings with the people in Civic Action and such. This has without a doubt been the most rewarding year of my life.

Love, .
Your Son, Fred

*   *   *

Most people who have been in combat and whose role involved killing the enemy, and in cases seeing them die, either need to make peace with those decisions before entering the military, during the actual war experience, or sometime afterwards. The rest of their lives can be weighed down by the memories of what they saw and did and how they felt about it. This is particularly problematic for Vietnam veterans who were fighting in a war that was waged with continually changing objectives, seemingly arbitrary rules of engagement, and some clear examples of questionable leadership and decision-making at the highest political levels. I have reflected on my own experience and asked whether there was anything I might have done differently to better prepare for this experience. I'm not sure that there was for me.

We were taught in combat infantry training to shoot weapons, to maintain them, to throw grenades, to put on gas masks, to escape and evade the enemy, to attack strategically, to move surreptitiously under fire, and techniques of hand-to-hand combat, etc. We were not taught that enemy soldiers had their own lives, their own goals and dreams, their own values and beliefs, their own love of country and passion to defend it, their own families they hoped to return to after the war.

Two people I know and respect had a son take his own life after service in combat in the U.S. Army in Afghanistan, personally experiencing some terrible encounters and struggling with PTSD after being honorably discharged from his military service. Their son was a writer, a sensitive young man who grew up in an idyllic rural island setting and entered the military with noble intentions. He found the actual experience of being a combat soldier to be very traumatic. They later published their son's war reflections in a book titled *A Soldier's Journal—Last Supper to No Goodbye*. They took their grief and turned it into a life quest to help veterans by forming an organization to help veterans dealing with PTSD and the effects of war to integrate back into their communities. They formed a community-based organization that is now known as the Whidbey Veterans Resource Center on Whidbey Island. It currently provides peer support groups that meet regularly, help to veterans in accessing their VA benefits, van transportation to city-based VA health care, and specialized counseling services for military veterans living on Whidbey Island.

Their personal recommendation at the culmination of the book project they completed in their son's memory was that young men and women not be allowed to enlist in the military until age 23 or 24. Their message was: "Stop taking the youngest into the military and into combat prior to them having their full human biological capacity to withstand the trauma of military experiences. We believe if we, civilians and veterans, carry these moral, physical, emotional, spiritual, and mental burdens of war together we will find our way to healing not only our veterans, but ourselves and our communities."

The military has recruited and drafted young men as young as 18, like my door gunner and friend, Paul Woodby, for military service, and many of them have benefited from the self-discipline, leadership opportunities, and organizational skills that come with military training. I was a young soldier at age 20. My experience in the military was a very positive one. I acknowledge that for some young people the experience can be profoundly different depending on the experiences they have and the people who are in their unit. I believe a need exists to inform young people of all of the risks and rewards of military service and to do as much as possible to see that they are comprehensively informed prior to their enlistment.

Soc Trang, Vietnam
Wednesday, October 30, 1968

Dear Mom, Dad, and Family,

I just returned from a relaxing 4-day pass at Vung Tau, a seaport town in the II Corps area. The town is very secure and the curfew at night is not until 11:00pm at which time you must be off the streets. The beaches are light brown sand with good surf and I spent the greater part of my time walking for miles up and down the beach, swimming, and soaking up the sun's rays. There are many large estates and modern villas of concrete and sandstone in the city proper and on the outlying drives along the ocean. The place is so secure and prosperous because the V.C. as well as U.S. soldiers find the town a relaxing break from the war. Many merchants are reaping immense profits from the fortunes of war.

There are quite a few con people, prostitution, and so forth. We had a blast going from bar to bar. I stayed in a villa that a friend of mine rents with his buddies who fly engineers out of the local airfield to construction sites throughout III and IV Corps. It was very modern, two story cement, with a rooftop patio which I found very relaxing at night for looking at the stars and a quiet place to think. What I appreciated most was getting in bed and being certain you weren't going to be mortared or scrambled but just a good sound sleep awaited you. And it was most enjoyable to walk down secure city streets in the day and at night without getting shot at or mortared.

Love,
Your Son,
Fred

Sidney, Australia
Thursday, October 31, 1968

Dear Mom, Dad, and Family,

I've started a few letters and then wham! Something else comes up to do here and the paper gets pushed aside. Tomorrow morning I return to good old Soc

Trang so tonight I'll give you a rundown of my many and varied activities over the past few days. All of the Australian people I have met are really great and go way out of their way to ensure that you have a very memorable 6 days. Incidentally it has without a doubt been the fastest 6 days in the last year at any rate. I met one girl at a mixer sponsored by the R & R center and on the next day we took the ferry to Manly Beach…. The day was cloudy because of the many wild bush fires that are burning in the open country on the outskirts of Sydney.

One day I took my camera into town and visited the New South Wales Art Gallery, Sydney Museum, and Hyde Park. Last night had a blind date with a nice girl and went to dinner at an Old Australian place that used to be an old prison, And we drank, ate, and sang old folk songs with an Australian Folk Band raising hell and dancing some really wild dances, you know just jumping up and down and clapping.

The country itself is geared down monetarily which is very interesting and appealing. The people drive smaller cars and people seem more concerned with one that runs good than owning the newest model with the latest accessories.

Love,
Your Son, Fred

Soc Trang, Vietnam
Sunday, November 17, 1968

Dear Mom, Dad, and Family,

Sunday morning, the sun is shining very brightly and all is well. I received notification of my next duty station. I'll be going to Fort Wolters in Texas and I really think it is about the best stateside assignment I could have gotten. The towns of Fort Worth and Dallas are within 60 miles with much to offer in the way of entertainment and many fine lakes in the area promise some good times. Also there are some very well-known fixed wing flight schools there and I'm sure I will get many chances to increase my pilot proficiency and gain additional ratings. You might mention the assignment to Mrs. Fleming I think I will probably be able to see Paul during Christmas leave but I would be all for going in on a real nice apartment.

Received a check from Spiegel Catalogues for $100.00 for the orphanage and will make plans for some type of Christmas party for the kids and use the rest to buy needed medical supplies and such. Looking forward to the package from Mrs. March and tell her thanks very much for her interest and generosity.

Love,
Your Son, Fred

Soc Trang, Vietnam
Tuesday, December 3, 1968

Dear Mom, Dad, and Family,

Well Everyone—I'm back at good old Soc Trang—on the last night of my stay in Sidney I was invited to dinner with a family who lived out in the suburbs. It was a very pleasant end to a really enjoyable R & R. Now I am getting shorter every day.

I'm flying firefly this week and the time is passing very quickly. I almost have a delay in route in the bag and am planning on a three or four day stop-over in Hawaii on the way home. I can't pass up the chance to see the country at Uncle Sam's expense. I should be home just before Christmas if all my plans work out as they should. I hope everything is going fine at home and see you soon.

Love,
Your Son,
Fred

*   *   *

As the days clicked down towards my DEROS (Date Estimated of Return from Over Seas) I was getting short, and the standard protocol was that you flew fewer missions and fewer combat assaults in the last couple of weeks of your tour. I was in the Tigers' Den one evening with just a few days left, enjoying some singing and having a few drinks with some Vikings and Tigers, and someone from operations came in and said, "We have a request for a couple of gunships to cover a medevac at Seven Canals. Someone there is wounded and in pretty bad shape and needs to be airlifted out of there tonight. We have Dustoff ready to go but they have been getting some action there today and there is a need for a couple of gunships to fly cover and escort the medevac in and out. Is anyone available to take it?"

I found myself raising my hand with three other Vikings, and before I knew it we were on the flight line cranking up the B models.

We touched base with each other and the Dustoff on the radios and took off in a flight of three for the area west of Soc Trang that we knew well as Seven Canals. We flew in a loose formation of three towards the area and decided that we would minimize the profiles of our aircraft by going in with lights off for the last mile or so.

We had radio contact with the outpost and could sense the expectation of the people on the ground to get this person some timely medical treatment. As I recall, it was a clear night with some light from the moon. We turned out the navigation lights, and the gunships settled into a circular pattern around the outpost. The Dustoff came in overhead and did a corkscrew-type approach down through the middle of our circular pattern and landed to a few flashlights at the outpost.

The wingman and I talked back and forth relaying our positions and watching out for the other aircraft. The Dustoff called "pacs loaded," and pulled pitch and called out his easterly heading setting out to return to Soc Trang. We kept our heads on a swivel and joined up with him in a loose V formation climbing up to 1,500 feet, turning the navigation lights back on, and following him back to Soc Trang. There wasn't any need for suppressive fire during the mission, but we couldn't help but think that, given the previous few days of reports from this outpost, that without the gun cover things might have gone a lot differently. That's how it was in the guns. Some days just the threat of a fully loaded gunship seemed to cause the VC to think twice about engaging a Dustoff helicopter. I'm glad they didn't pick this night to change that pattern of behavior. Later that night, I was glad I took the mission even though my days in-country were now numbered on a couple of hands.

As my days wound down towards my DEROS, I went to Can Tho. I stopped in the MACV office to get paperwork for taking a captured Chinese Communist Mauser rifle home as a war souvenir. Upon returning from R&R in Australia with about a month left of my in-country tour of duty, I began the paperwork process of getting ready to leave Vietnam. Headquarters for the First Aviation Brigade was in Can Tho. On a day when I was not scheduled to fly missions, I hopped in a UH-ID slick as a passenger and then inquired about the routing for the flight home. To my delight one of the routes home for the contracted commercial airliners had a stop in Hawaii for fuel and passengers. I began the process of requesting to be on this particular flight.

When it came time for me to depart Vietnam, a similar process of departure was in effect but now consisted of getting on a C-123 (a U.S. Air Force transport) in Soc Trang and riding to Tan Son Nhut Air Base and then transferring to a commercial airliner. When I arrived in Hawaii, I decided to rent a motor scooter to see the island and rode out to a secluded beach. I marveled at the beautiful beach and jumped in the water to be taken out rather quickly over my head by a strong undertow. As I struggled to get back to the sandy beach, my thought process was, "I have survived a year in Vietnam and now I am on the verge of drowning in the waters off Hawaii." Just by luck I got deposited back near the shore by the next couple of waves and decided there were other dangers in life that were just as life-threatening as combat.

I got a room in the BOQ (Billeted Officers Quarters) at Hickam Air Force Base and got scheduled on a military flight a few days later in an old Air Force transport two-engine plane called Old Shakey, a C-124 flying from Hickam to McChord Air Force Base in Tacoma, Washington, where I had grown up and where many of my uncles, aunts, and cousins lived. The plane was a cargo plane, and the flight engineer showed me how to strap into a cot that was suspended from the interior side of the plane amidst a cargo of jet engines and other mechanical equipment. In the air I was encouraged to stay in the cot but could walk around if necessary. The flight took about 13 hours as I recall and didn't go more than 13,000 feet over the ocean. I had a window by my cot that looked out at the flames shooting about eight feet out of the exhaust stacks on the radial engines. The weather was clear, the moon was out and the flight was smooth. At McChord Air Force Base, I found a phone and called my uncle Jerry Harnish, and he came out to meet me and take me to his house to stay over while my parents came from Seattle to pick me up. It was the end of a great adventure for me.

16

Reflecting on Vietnam

I was a very average student academically in high school, and my personal interest in the subject of history was even more limited. Many of the facts I have learned more recently were not common knowledge in my peer group at the time I entered the Army. They were not the regular topic of high school students' conversations in the seminary.

When I enlisted in the U.S. Army in Seattle, Washington, on December 6, 1966, I was 20 years old and interested in learning to fly helicopters, having an adventure, serving my country, and being a warrant officer in the U.S. Army. I also believed I would be contributing in a very personal way to fighting the spread of Communism throughout the world and helping the people of South Vietnam establish a democratic government for the people of the Republic of South Vietnam.

Indochina had a long history of French control and war with its neighbors. Japan had invaded various parts of the country of French Indochina in 1940. The Japanese did not establish a Japanese government but decided to align themselves with the pro–Nazi French Vichy government. The Japanese chose to work under the leadership of the French and committed their military advisors to be in a secondary administrative role in the country. As World War II came to a close in Europe in March of 1945, the Nazi influence was defeated, and the Japanese began an open resistance to the French-Vichy government and set about establishing a state government with a puppet emperor named Bao Dai.

In the spring of 1945, American involvement in Indochina came in the form of military hardware, guns, ammunition, and training for military advisors from the Office of Strategic Services (known as the OSS), the precursor to the U.S. Central Intelligence Agency. This military support was provided to a small band of freedom fighters known as the Viet Minh who were at the time waging guerrilla warfare against the Japanese in northern Vietnam. These fighters were led by two men, Ho Chi Minh and Vo Nguyen Giap, in skirmishes near the Chinese border.

Fredrik Logevall, a Pulitzer prize-winning author, in his book *Embers of War: The Fall of an Empire and the Making of America's Vietnam*, characterized the Vietnamese people as having a very positive perception of Ho Chi Minh from their personal interactions with advisors from the Office of Strategic Services, who invariably described him as "warm, intelligent, and keen to cooperate with the United States."

Ho Chi Minh stated, "American technicians could help build an independent Vietnam." Ho Chi Minh was a student of American history and saw his Viet Minh's resistance as akin to the American Revolution and his role similar to that of George Washington in his efforts to achieve determination and democratic government in the United States of America.

President Franklin D. Roosevelt, in a meeting with Winston Churchill and Chiang Kai-shek of the Republic of China in 1944, stated, "Indochina should not go back to France…. France has had the country and its thirty million inhabitants for nearly one hundred years and the people are worse off than they were in the beginning…. The people of Indochina are entitled to something better than that."

Mr. Logevall further asserted that, "after World War II, Ho Chi Minh tried to get American support in the fight against the French (occupation) of Vietnam. After World War II, Ho Chi Minh wrote at least 8 letters that were never answered to United States President Harry Truman asking for American help. Ho played down his communist background and hinted that he would welcome U.S. investment in a free Vietnam and that he was open to considering allowing the United States to set up a military naval base in Vietnam. The letters apparently went unanswered. Soviet allies were growing and expanding in countries like Iran and Turkey and were becoming a major threat. People were afraid of communist world domination."

Two incidents prompted the U.S. commitment to support France after World War II. One occurred in August of 1949 when the Soviets conducted a first successful test of a nuclear weapon. A second occurred in October of 1949 when the Chinese Communists defeated the Nationalists and took full Communist control of China. Later, as we know, Ho Chi Minh aligned his Viet Minh with the Communists, and his leadership of the Viet Minh was a major factor in the defeat of the French at the defining battle of Dien Bien Phu in 1954 where the French experienced a devastating defeat and surrender.

What might have happened if President Truman had responded to the letters? Did the fear of Communist domination of the world, so present at that time throughout the world, set the stage for the unfolding events that resulted in the Vietnam War?

It has been revealed that Richard M. Nixon lied to President Lyndon B. Johnson and took advantage of the timely opportunity to quietly delay the Paris peace talks so that he could become president of the United States of

America. Nixon maintained that he had not undermined President Johnson's 1968 peace initiative to bring the war in Vietnam to a conclusion during his term of office. "My God. I would never do anything to encourage [North Vietnam] not to come to the table," Nixon told Johnson, in a phone conversation that was recorded on the White House taping system. In later released documents, H.R. "Bob" Haldeman, Nixon's aide, revealed that Nixon had directed him, and in turn his campaign staffs' efforts, to undermine the Paris peace talks because he thought this could give him a leg up over his opponent, Vice President Hubert H. Humphrey, in the 1968 election. On October 22, 1968, in advance of the November 3 elections, he had ordered Mr. Haldeman to move forward in this manner.

Former general Pete Piotrowski published a shocking accusation in his book *Basic Airman to General: The Secret War & Other Conflicts: Lessons in Leadership & Life*, stating "that the U.S. notified the North Vietnamese government of U.S. airstrikes ahead of time." This fact was confirmed in later years in an interview with Dean Rusk, secretary of state at the time. He stated in the interview, "We didn't want to harm the North Vietnamese people and so we passed the targets to the Swiss embassy in Washington that would be bombed the next day with instructions to pass them on to the NVN government through their embassy in Hanoi."

These examples of political ineptitude at the highest levels of government are astonishing in that this kind of thinking surely did at least two major things. One, it enabled the North Vietnamese to not only move civilians out of the area but also, more importantly, move anti-aircraft weapons into the area ready to shoot down the Navy and Air Force fighters on their doomed missions. I wonder how many POWs were held in the Hanoi Hilton, having been shot down as a direct result of this particular ill-conceived strategy. Secondly, then candidate Nixon's efforts to delay the Paris peace talks for political reasons in the presidential elections was an equally egregious act.

* * *

After World War II, the French attempted to reinstate their colonial rule over the Indochinese countries of Vietnam, Cambodia, and Laos. They asked for support from the United States, who had been their ally in World War II, to help them in this pursuit. Ho Chi Minh, as was stated earlier, also tried at the end of the war to get support from the United States. It is left to speculation whether outspoken and passionate administrative supporters of the French, fearful of the spread of Communism, kept Ho from meeting with the president. There was enormous pressure at the time to side with the French in supporting colonial rule of Vietnam, and a growing fear emerged as Ho Chi Minh's efforts were characterized as being associated with an expanding Soviet and Communist movement to systematically take over the free world country by country, starting with Vietnam, Cambodia and Laos.

In early 1950, five years after the end of World War II, the Truman administration decided to provide financial aid to the French military in Indochina. The ostensible goal of this move was to contain the spread of communism throughout the world. President Truman was advised by Secretary of State Dean Acheson to give France military and financial aid to oppose the Communists and the Democratic Republic of Vietnam, the name of the emerging movement to form a free and independent nation of Vietnam. Nationalist China had fallen to the Communists, and Communist China had mobilized troops on the Indochina border the previous winter. The Soviet Union and Communist China followed by acknowledging Ho Chi Minh as the emerging leader of the government of Vietnam. China also began to train and supply military weapons to the Viet Minh, who began identifying themselves as the Revolutionary League for the Independence of Vietnam and were, at the time, developing into a major military resistance force.

Top U.S. officials informed the president that they would either have to support the legal government in Indochina or face the spread of communism in Southeast Asia. In May of 1950, President Truman officially authorized the use of U.S. funds to back the French in their war against Ho Chi Minh and the Viet Minh.

The French increasingly re-established control in Vietnam over the next four years. This prompted resistance from and growth of the Viet Minh. Many began to say the French owned the country in the day and the Viet Minh owned the country in the night as the resistance of the Viet Minh was widely supported and largely an underground guerrilla type of resistance. French soldiers were brutal in their ruthless re-establishment of colonial control. The French maintained they were supporting and protecting the largely Catholic population of Vietnam from the evils associated with communism. But in their enthusiasm for domination they burned villages deemed to be uncooperative, executed resistors, raped women, and promulgated an atmosphere of fear throughout the country.

The legacy of United States support to its ally France in the form of finances and military advisors was carried on and grew significantly through the succession of presidents from President Truman to President Eisenhower, himself a former general in World War II. Animosities built between the French and resisting Viet Minh until a defining battle that occurred in 1954 at Dien Bien Phu.

By 1953, the French had lost 100,000 troops in Vietnam and were no further along on their plan for "pacification" of the country than when they started in 1945. Ho Chi Minh was growing in his prominence among his people. General Giap had become a military co-leader with Ho Chi Minh and was much more aggressive in his beliefs and tactics. He proposed a strategic plan to wipe out the French and turn the tide of the war. General Giap surreptitiously moved 250,000 Viet Minh troops, 200 large guns, and related material into position around the mountaintop stronghold at Dien Bien Phu. On March 13, 1954, the fighting began with the Viet Minh shelling the French stronghold. The French appealed to President Eisenhower for more military and material support. He consulted with the British and ultimately declined the request. A 55-day brutal battle ensued. On May 7, 1954, the French, whose numbers had been decimated by 8,000 men, surrendered. General Giap and the Viet Minh emerged victorious, though the price they paid in war dead was a heavy one, estimated to be 24,000 men. The end of French colonialism in Vietnam was signaled by this surrender.

Vietnam was divided at the 17th parallel into North and South Vietnam, elections were planned and Ho Chi Minh was considered to be a clear favorite to lead a reunified Vietnam in the future. Dien Bien Phu underscored the resolve of the Viet Minh and their leaders. This battle and defeat was now a matter of history and one that was seemingly forgotten or never internalized by the politicians who charted the course for later involvement of the United States in the future internal struggles for Vietnam.

The proposed open and free elections were neither open nor free. A leader, Ngo Dinh Diem, emerged based in Saigon, promising democracy and hatred for the French and communism, but his management style followed and incorporated a crime-type syndicate characterized by corruption that was pervasive in the country. The French withdrew completely. The idea of reunification of the split country was abandoned.

President Eisenhower met with Diem, and this meeting lent credibility to Diem's leadership. President Eisenhower began sending advisors to Vietnam ostensibly to "win the hearts and minds of the people." The Viet Minh began killing corrupt officials who were tyrannical in their leadership styles as the country began disintegrating into chaos with a series of coups and military leaders.

President John F. Kennedy came into office as the situation in Vietnam was further unraveling. Advisors continued to be placed in Vietnam throughout the fifties and sixties. He put pressure on Diem to resign or be replaced and even approved a coup effort. Then in 1963 President Kennedy himself was assassinated. After his death he would be quoted as saying, "I shouldn't have approved of the coup." All of this dysfunction set the stage for involvement of the United States in Vietnam.

* * *

I had joined the Army in December of 1966. I was excited to learn how to fly helicopters and felt strongly that I could make a difference with my life in helping the Vietnamese form a democratic form of government. I believed we were fighting to address the spread of Communism throughout the free world. In learning more about the history of war in Vietnam, I had an aha moment when I realized that the Tet Offensive of 1968, the deadliest year of the war, when I served there, was probably an attempted re-enactment of the successful victory of the Viet Minh over the French at Dien Bien Phu.

After my tour in Vietnam I returned stateside to an assignment in Mineral Wells, Texas, teaching weather- and flight-related subjects to warrant officer candidates and regular officers at the Primary Helicopter Training Center at Fort Wolters, Texas. This was an enjoyable assignment for me. I lived with two other Vietnam veterans in an apartment in Fort Worth with a swimming pool in the shape of the state of Texas. We each had a muscle car. Paul had a Pontiac GTO, Frank had an Oldsmobile 442, and I had a Corvette. We enjoyed an active social life in Fort Worth and Dallas on the weekends.

A year later, I asked for and was granted an early release from the military and I returned to Washington and re-entered the seminary. My thoughts at the time were to become a priest and serve as an Army chaplain. I continued my interest in military flying by becoming a member of the 540th Assault Helicopter Company at Fort Lewis, Washington, with the Washington State National Guard, where I flew Hueys, OH-23 Ravens, and CH-34 Choctaws while pursuing seminary training. I retained my military classification as a helicopter gunship pilot. This created some pushback at the seminary from one priest/teacher in particular who was actively involved in a number of war protests in downtown Seattle and thought it was inconsistent with the mission of Saint Thomas Seminary to have a seminarian like me be active in a military unit. I could sense his disapproval as I walked out on Fridays with my flight helmet, etc., and he was also departing to a war protest in Seattle.

This was another time of discernment for me and of processing my Vietnam experiences. Returning to the seminary was quite an interesting experience. The enrollment in the seminary was decimated during the 1960s and there were only 40 students remaining in the major seminary training to become priests in the Archdiocese of Seattle. My leadership and combat experience in Vietnam taught me to question, listen, and do whatever was necessary to get the job done. This sort of "can-do" attitude appealed to many of my classmates, and when a specific question about the quality of the food surfaced, I was elected to go express the concerns of the student body to the administration and ask for some changes in our food and meals. When a mere meeting resulted in the desired changes, I was elevated to student body president and began being seen as the "go-to person" for solving student dissatisfaction issues. This was quite a change from the way I was perceived in my previous seminary life.

At the end of the year, things were further unraveling and a number of students were discussing the possibility of leaving the school. I personally questioned my vocation and decided to enter a state university and become a teacher. I withdrew and entered Central Washington University (then Central Washington State College) and subsequently completed a BA and a master's degree in education. While at CWU, I read every book I could find on the teaching profession and especially on early childhood education. I volunteered in a small parochial school in town in exchange for being able to do some of my practicum activities and assignments with the students there.

Halfway through my second year at Saint Andrew's School, a teaching position opened at the second-grade level. I took it and finished out the year teaching in the school. Toward the end of the year, I applied for a permanent position teaching kindergarten on the west side of the state, in the growing Marysville School District. As the year ended, the older parish priest, who was straight from Ireland, called me in and said, "Since June was not a full month, we are not paying people for June."

I responded, "Well, Father, that isn't the way it works in America. I think I should be paid even though the month was a partial month."

He said, "You know that we are closing the school and the convent. Would you take the dining room furniture in the convent for your pay?"

I thought the furniture was quite nice and agreed. That furniture was part of our lives for another 10 years or so.

I was hired under a Title I federal grant in western Washington, in the growing suburban Marysville School District north of Seattle, to be a kindergarten teacher. I commented to my supervisor, Frank Carlson, who had hired me, that I thought the grant for the program could be written differently and better meet the needs of parents and students. He saw a need in the growing school district for someone to write and manage grants for the district, and this path led me to become the district's grants manager and ultimately the assistant superintendent for curriculum and instruction and later finance and operations. Frank Carlson and I became great friends, and I will always appreciate the fact that he hired me, one of the few men at the time who was interested in teaching kindergarten. I look back on my years in Marysville as very special. I met my wife, Shannon, through a friend, Mary Schau, who worked there and initially told me about the job posting. Mary and her husband, Ed, a classmate of mine from the seminary, have been great friends over the years.

In the middle of my education career, after completing a doctorate in educational administration at age 50, I was eligible for early retirement and became the principal and development director of a small and unique private Catholic school in the Wallingford neighborhood in the city of Seattle. It served children in preschool through grade 8. I held this position from 1998 to 2005, and it was a memorable and very rewarding experience. I was hired for this position by an extraordinary priest who was the parish pastor, Father Paul Waldie. The school was in a bit of turmoil from the leadership of the principal and he wanted me to restore its reputation, improve student performance, and put the school on a firm financial footing. I was a parish member and helped the school raise funds to operate while I was completing my doctoral studies at Seattle Pacific University.

17

Historical Lessons Learned

The Vietnam War is going down in history as one of the most controversial and misunderstood wars in the history of wars fought by the military of the United States of America. I believe we owe it to ourselves as citizens of this country to learn some lessons for the future from each war effort that we make a decision to enter. My thoughts and reflections about this area of personal interest for me come from five perspectives: (1) political leadership, (2) military leadership, (3) combat soldier, (4) morality, and (5) historical context.

From a political leadership perspective, the involvement of the United States government in Vietnam seemed rooted in a widely held belief among the citizenry that democracy was fundamentally the noblest form of government. Many Americans believed democracy and the right of self-determination were basic human rights that man by his very nature was destined to pursue. Additionally, many of those who ascribe to this belief believed that communism was fundamentally a repressive and regressive form of government that controlled the individual citizen and subjugated individual needs to the needs of the state. These beliefs set the stage for a convincing view that all people around the world would be better off if they were governed in a democratic manner than if they were governed based from a different set of assumptions like the communist perspective. Our country had taken great pride in its history and foundational principles. Many other countries looked to the United States of America as a model for how a democratic government should be constituted and function.

Problems surfaced when our country and in particular its political leaders came to the conclusion that other countries would be more successful if they were led as a democratic form of government without taking into consideration their culture, history, and developmental stage of readiness to accept the challenges associated with forming and operating this type of government.

When we stood up with our allies against the obvious evils of unbridled military aggression and basic human rights violations during World

War II, our strength and principles were celebrated around the world. We let that previous experience influence our later decision-making to the degree that we responded with support for France, our ally from World War II, in its effort to reinstate colonial leadership over Vietnam after that war. We missed the opportunity to acknowledge the limitations and dark sides of colonial oppression. When our political leaders ignored the requests and attempts to communicate with our government that came from an emerging leader of the people within Vietnam, Ho Chi Minh, to support self-determination efforts in Vietnam, we lost a defining moment and the opportunity to help a fledgling nation move from colonial oppression to build a better system of governance espoused by their populace and emerging leaders of the time. Those decisions led us down a path of deeper and deeper involvement in the Vietnam War to bolster up South Vietnamese forces that were ill prepared for the task at hand and not representative of the emerging popular leadership of the country.

There were defining moments where we might have seen the course of history change and have avoided escalating America's involvement in the Vietnam War. Ho Chi Minh made multiple attempts to communicate with President Truman. One source documented 13 letters that were written to President Truman but were never seen by him. In these letters, Ho Chi Minh expressed his feeling that he was similar in his beliefs to our Founding Fathers. He alluded to aligning his efforts with the United States and actually intimated that a U.S. Navy base might be located in a reconstituted and reorganized Vietnam. History tells us that the letters were never read by the president, and we are left to speculate whether cabinet-level administrators with conflicting agendas caused this to happen.

The Vietnam War had its beginnings for the United States in the 1950s, when President Eisenhower authorized military advisors to help the country address the challenges presented by emerging unethical leadership in the governance of Vietnam after the French defeat at Dien Bien Phu. When the free and open elections that occurred in 1954 were neither free nor open in the way they were conducted, a journey down a path destined for failure began for American military advisors in Vietnam. ARVN troops and their military leaders did not take up the gauntlet of war with a deep commitment to victory and based on strongly held beliefs and core values. They had been at war in one form or another for over 100 years, and they were neither inspired by their corrupt leaders nor convinced of their ability to put their own needs above the corruption and shortsighted desires for power and the trappings of success. The actions of the military leaders were not seen by the people as being noble and well-intentioned but as self-serving and personally enriching their families while the common citizen's life was expendable.

American military leaders, who approached the war first as advisors and then from the perspective of winning battles and skirmishes, became concerned about the lack of success of the advisor/advisee relationship with the Army of the Republic of Vietnam. In response to lack of success in various engagements, they requested and received more military personnel and led them into deeper and deeper military roles as the Vietnamese military showed itself to be not up to the task at hand. This resulted in increased bombing and use of primarily American backed and executed military maneuvers and logistics and choosing metrics like body counts and territory taken as indicators of success.

The war was reported over television on a daily basis to Americans back in the United States, by reporters embedded with both South Vietnamese and United States military units. The atrocities of war were many, and these were shown in graphic detail to an American citizenry who lost confidence that the strategies were well conceived or having the desired results. As military leaders became more and more frustrated with the lack of military discipline in the South Vietnamese Army, there was a tendency to overcompensate with escalated American efforts in battles, use of aircraft bombing, defoliation of major portions of the country, and increasing use of ordnance and military power. Body counts became the accepted metric for evaluating skirmishes and engagements. The North Vietnamese and Viet Cong body counts were regularly reported as being much greater than the American losses, and they probably were. Remember that in the defining colonial oppression battle at Dien Bien Phu, the Vietnamese won the battle by sacrificing an estimated 24,000 lives to the 8,000 given by the French prior to surrender. The Vietnamese were not limited to thinking about their engagement in war as being evaluated with body counts.

Our logic in Vietnam became that if their side lost more men in a battle than ours that was a win for our side. Of course, the North Vietnamese and Viet Cong did not have the military hardware and ordnance to equal the seemingly endless support of the American military. What they lacked in hardware and armament they compensated for in passion for their purpose, ingenuity in guerrilla warfare tactics, and commitment to the end goal of their cause. In the final analysis, the North Vietnamese and Viet Cong were more passionate about their cause of self-determination and permanent escape from further colonial domination than their South Vietnamese counterparts were about their beliefs in democratic processes prevailing over a communist form of governance. The corrupt and self-serving leadership legacy that appeared endemic in the South Vietnamese government was a significant factor in undermining the credibility of the nobility of the democratic approach to governance.

These war efforts were escalated in the 1960s by President Kennedy, continued to expand under presidents Johnson and Nixon, and were brought to closure under President Ford. On April 30, 1975, the Vietnam War was brought to a rather ignominious and hasty closure, as viewed by many Vietnam veterans, that included tactically and strategically embarrassing actions led by an ambassador in a questionable mental state, who failed to accept the impending defeat of the Army of the Republic of Vietnam's military and overthrow of the South Vietnamese military leadership in Saigon. This was followed by a precipitous withdrawal of military personnel and the abandonment of many South Vietnamese who had been loyal supporters of American involvement in the war. These people left behind were subjected to persecution, imprisonment, and their own devices for evasion and escape to freedom from retaliation and retribution at the hands of the North Vietnamese and their counterinsurgent arm, the Viet Cong.

As the war progressed, various military actions were taken that seemed to lack focus or purpose and be characterized by metrics like inflated body counts or reports of accomplishments designed to show that the United States backed ARVN forces were winning, when in fact they were seemingly unmotivated or lacking enthusiasm for the causes being pursued. The war seemed to be undertaken for noble but shortsighted reasons, conducted and managed with serious misperceptions and questionable actions, and brought to closure seemingly without a plan for strategic withdrawal or protection of personnel or asset recovery. The challenge for the combat soldiers in Vietnam was that they were fighting in an unconventional war that often did not make sense to them. Troops became dispirited over time after taking and retaking the same objective in the same area multiple times with loss of life, and then relinquishing the area to the same situation that existed before the battle or skirmish. There is no question that frequently a combat soldier approaches a new engagement with renewed aggression if the previous engagement resulted in the loss of the lives of friends around him.

Tragedies like My Lai, where a specific unit was led to perpetuate unspeakable atrocities, were an ever-present possibility and easy for even the most ethical person to justify from a logical point of view, in that every encounter with the enemy could reveal a suicide bomber or passionate opponent who believed that dying for the cause was a legitimate action. Hanoi Hannah broadcast that the Blue Diamond Devils of the Delta would get theirs for wreaking havoc on the Viet Cong in the Delta. Rumors abounded that women and children were co-opted into being willing to give their lives for the cause or that bounties were placed on taking out a helicopter pilot or aircraft. They also included stories of bodies of flight crewmembers being discovered having been mutilated, and one story of unexplained aircraft explosions due to grenades being placed in the gas tanks with a rubber band around the detonation device so that when the fuel ate through it the grenade would explode in the gas tank and obliterate the aircraft. The challenge for the combat soldier was to carry out the mission while exercising the responsibilities of commanding the flight crew of a helicopter to follow rules of engagement and specific orders given for each mission. It was essential for a person to have a set of personal core values and operating principles that were adhered to for being at peace later in life with the decisions made in combat situations.

*   *   *

It was obvious to the combat soldier that corruption plagued the leadership of the South Vietnamese military and drove much of the economy in South Vietnam. American military supplies were available in the PX but also on the black market. Prostitution and drugs were commonly available and the currency in the country was changed randomly in an attempt to thwart the black-market profits and trade. A picture emerged of a country destined for failure that was unraveling due to a lack of ethical and moral leadership.

It was important for the pilots in command in our unit to know the difference between legal authority and doing the right and moral thing. For example, a Vietnamese province chief had the authority to declare an area a free-fire zone. That meant that the area was so sympathetic to the Viet Cong that any person observed could be assumed to be a combatant and engaged. This was all of the legal authority that a flight crew needed to engage observed personnel. A few pilots took this literally and let their crewmembers engage whomever they saw. Most pilots adhered to a belief system that had strict criteria for flight crews to discharge weapons, such as (1) if fired upon; (2) if engaged in a combat assault and directed to fire on approach or departure from or to a combat landing zone or operational area to "keep their heads down"; (3) if ordered to use recon by fire to see if an aircraft could engage the enemy or discover hidden caches of ordnance or weapons from secondary explosions, like rockets fired into suspicious-looking hooches; (4) when entering an obviously engaged combat situation; (5) when discovering combatants dressed in military uniforms or black clothing with weapons upon previously given orders to do so or as given orders from a command and control aircraft officer in the area.

The country of Vietnam, like many countries, had a long history of being at war. They were steeped in a tradition of war and military service. They had been invaded by neighboring countries and had been occupied as a colony by the French for many years. They had a religious tradition based on Buddhism and had been also heavily influenced by Catholicism during the French colonial period. These two religious perspectives were often at odds with each other, and conflicts existed between them and the people who supported them.

When Vietnam was invaded by neighbors, the Vietnamese people developed an approach to warfare that took advantage of their knowledge of their homeland and their ability to be long-suffering and endure significant hardships in a quest for nation building and self-determination. This approach evolved over time from one of primitive fighting with basic weaponry into a contemporary sophisticated model of guerrilla warfare that included traditional and non-traditional weapons and tactics. An insight into the resolve and commitment of the Vietnamese people can be deduced from their sacrifices made while battling the French. They were creative and tactical as they surreptitiously positioned people and weapons around the French stronghold at Dien Bien Phu. The French underestimated their resolve and capacity for waging war. A similar end came to the Vietnam War as North Vietnamese and Viet Cong troops encircled and overran Saigon.

18

The Just War Theory
and Vietnam

A number of philosophers, historians, and Church leaders have shaped the "just war theory" over the centuries. Some unique dimensions of the Vietnam War prompted a new generation of philosophical and theoretical thought, reflection, and interpretation of this important theory.

Scholars and early students of history attributed the beginnings of the traditional just war theory to Saint Augustine (354 to 430 AD). Saint Augustine is considered one of the primary architects of Western thought. He was born in the town of Tagaste in North Africa. At the age of 29, he left North Africa and settled in Rome during the decline of the Roman Empire and rise of Christianity. Rome was under siege from various tribes from the north and east. Christians were struggling with what military response to these invaders was permitted by their faith. Augustine had been chosen to be the Bishop of Hippo. In this role he sought to lead his people and to answer many questions posed by the early Christians and in particular the defining questions related to war and military service. One question was: "Can a Christian answer the empire's call to military duty and still have a clear conscience before God?" His reflections included some fundamental premises that became the foundational assumptions of the traditional just war theory for the emerging Roman Catholic Church.

Thomas Aquinas (1225 to 1274 BCE) was born in southern Italy, was taught by Benedictine monks at Monte Cassino, studied at Cologne under Saint Albert the Great, and achieved a doctorate at the University of Paris. He was a theologian and a philosopher. He formatted the reflections of Augustine into specific criteria that remain the basis for the just war theory as it has been defined in the Roman Catholic Church today. In his work *Summa Theologica* he organizes, categorizes, and explains the elements of the just war theory.

According to the just war theory, the morality of a war is tested in two parts. These two parts are defined with two Latin-termed categories. One is *jus ad bellum* (justice to war)—the conditions for justly going to war. The second is *jus in bello* (justice in war)—the conditions for the just conduct of a war. From this traditional philosophical perspective, wars are judged twice, first with reference to the reasons for initiating them and secondly with reference to the means adopted in actually fighting them.

According to *jus ad bellum*, a just war, at its outset, must have just authority, just cause, just intention, and be a last resort. *Jus in bello* stipulates that a just war, as it is conducted, must have proportionality, discrimination, and responsibility.

A number of philosophers and researchers have concluded that the Vietnam War was not a just war because their view inextricably linked *jus ad bellum* with *jus in bello* in their interpretation of the just war theory. Many of these philosophers and researchers have never been a combatant in a war, and therefore their views are not supported by primary-source experience. I have read a few doctoral dissertations that have come to this conclusion.

Mr. Michael Walzer, author of the seminal book *Just and Unjust Wars: A Moral Argument with Historical Illustrations,* is a scholar and author whose writings have been referenced frequently in analyses of the Vietnam War. There are some very valuable insights from his work, first regarding the responsibility of the United States and its leaders, both political and military, and second regarding the unique role of the combat soldier in war. Mr. Walzer's research is based not only in philosophy and morality but also in military history, the gathering of personal combat stories, novels and poems, and in some factors and insights unique to the role of the combat soldier. He was not a combat soldier himself but has expanded his view and perspective beyond other academics of the just war theory from this additional research.

The Vietnam War began in the 1950s with advisors under President Eisenhower, was escalated in the 1960s under President Kennedy, and continued under Presidents Johnson, Nixon, and Ford. The Vietnam War was brought to an ignominious closure on April 30, 1975. From this perspective the war lasted some 10 to 20 years. Communism was widely perceived to be a very real threat to democracies around the world. Communist countries represented themselves as wanting to expand their span of control and take over other countries. There was an international belief in the "domino theory," that neighboring countries were like dominoes set on end in close proximity to each other and if one fell to communism, they would all fall into communist domination like dominoes. The principles of communism were considered inconsistent with Western beliefs in freedom, liberty, and justice for all.

There may have been limited knowledge of the extent of the corruption that plagued the leadership of South Vietnam and that it would accelerate and continue to unravel. However, it is plausible that the evolving pattern of corruption that emerged and grew unabated painted a picture of a country destined for failure. As the war progressed, various actions were taken politically and strategically to respond to emerging levels of awareness. As dissatisfaction with tactics mounted, and a number of events unfolded in sequence, what resulted was that the war took on enough distorted dimensions, and was concurrently misdirected by advisors to the presidents at the highest government levels.

In my opinion, the war was undertaken for noble but shortsighted reasons, and the way it was conducted and managed, with serious misperceptions and questionable actions, resulted in a war that was brought to closure in a such a manner that it no longer met the second criteria of the just war theory.

As Michael Walzer states, once you are involved at the combat soldier level, these leadership and political issues become secondary to the role of being a combat soldier. Your role in its simplest form is to kill the enemy. Their role is to kill you. This is a frightening realization that all combat soldiers come to and are charged with doing.

The soldiers I knew for the most part believed that they were involved in a cause so noble that they were willing to risk their lives on a daily basis to fight the war. The leadership I witnessed at the company and platoon level was both enlightened and informed and responsive to the commands that were given from higher-ups. The cause, at the outset, was curtailing the spread of communism throughout the world. I decided for myself that I did believe in the war, that I would do my very best to do the difficult work of a combat helicopter pilot, with the information and awareness of the factors at stake in waging the war and based on the information I had available to me at the time.

My awareness has been expanded in the later years of my life with the disclosures of decisions made at both the political levels and the strategic levels that were less than honorably motivated. I am deeply saddened about these revelations and for the deaths of soldiers on all sides of this conflict. I acknowledge, like the song says, that I was indeed a weapon in the Vietnam War. It was a war intensely fought by courageous soldiers on all sides. I was one of those soldiers.

I worked in the Marysville School District for 24 years and in three other public school districts as an administrator for six more. Early on in my time in Marysville, a very skilled superintendent and leader of the district saw the power of a staff development program called "Increasing Human Effectiveness." Dick Huselton encouraged all staff to participate in the program and selected teams consisting of a classified and a certified person to teach the concepts of this program to all employees in the district for college credit. Ultimately, we had about 400 employees trained in this program.

The human potential movement was gaining support across the country, and we were seeing some exciting results right in our district when people began to realize how much of a difference they could make not only in their chosen profession of education but in their personal lives, as well. Some of the dimensions in the program were awareness, self-image, self-esteem, self-talk, visualization, goal setting, making and managing change, and achieving your personal and professional goals and dreams one day at a time.

The concepts really struck a chord with me, and I began to implement them in my personal and professional life. In one of the visioning activities, I set a number of personal and professional goals. I was surprised by how much progress I was able to make and the power of writing these goals down, making a plan to accomplish them, and knowing how to take steps each day that led me in the direction of a more satisfying and rewarding life. The enthusiastic program author and presenter, Mr. Bob Moawad, personally presented to those of us chosen to be on one of the leadership/ trainer teams, and he encouraged us to not place limits on our thinking but to realize the tremendous potential we all had for unlimited personal and professional growth and success.

I found that this training helped me not only in my work and personal life, but in my thinking about the experiences I had had in combat in Vietnam. I learned that most people's thoughts are predominantly negative and how powerful just changing your thoughts could be. It was a transformational process for me personally and it came at a time—"a teachable moment"—when I was in a particularly receptive mode for internalizing this material.

One activity involved creating a personal list of all of the things you might like to accomplish if you looked at your life as having no limits on what you could accomplish. This is a very empowering activity that few people ever engage in during their lifetime. For most people, their lives unfold in a random manner, and their perception is that some people are just lucky and others unlucky and that determines their success or failure in life. I listed the following accomplishments I would like to see: achieve financial independence; get a doctoral degree; become a superintendent of schools; hold public office; teach college; write a book; travel; have interesting hobbies; maintain a spiritual dimension in my life; have positive relationships; become a national-level presenter; achieve a high degree of physical fitness and lead a healthy lifestyle; travel; become an expert in a certain area of my work; be a happy person; make a difference in the quality of life for others; be a good friend to my friends; be a positive influence in my family and have a satisfying family life; be a good parent; own an airplane, boat, motorcycle, and log cabin; play the guitar and entertain friends, family and others, etc. I wasn't sure how I would accomplish all of it, but it was exciting just listing the possibilities of a "no limit thinking" life. A review of my résumé in my golden years is empowering because I have had the joy of accomplishing these goals and many others along the way that I had not ever dreamed I could accomplish. I attribute a lot of my success to the power of positive thinking and to the strategies I learned in Human Effectiveness training. My sincere thanks go out to my friend, mentor, and visionary superintendent, Dick Huselton, and Bob Moawad (RIP) and his Human Effectiveness training program that has enriched my life immeasurably.

The VA has rated me as a 50 percent disabled Vietnam veteran for service-related conditions. I am a very active person. I have been blessed to lead a very productive, active, and satisfying life from my point of view. When I was evaluated with a number of assessments at the VA hospital in 2012 as part of my registering in the VA health care system, I was intrigued by the comprehensiveness of the assessments and examinations. At the time my interest was in registering with the VA while I had my faculties about me as a pre-emptive measure for potential issues later in life when filling out forms and gathering data would be challenging.

Thirty percent of my assigned disabilities are attributed to moderate to severe damage to disks in my neck and back. I am in the Agent Orange registry and flew gunship cover on defoliation missions where we were around the stuff in the loading areas and flew below and behind the spray ship. I have been diagnosed with peripheral neuropathy involving my extremities (hands and feet). I also have been tested for hearing loss related to combat noise and have high-tech hearing aids provided by the VA that interface with my iPhone.

On my own and separate from the VA, I had a laminectomy in 2014 with titanium plates and screws that hold together the lower part of my back. I had this operation after a few bouts with pinched nerves and compromised disks resulted in significant pain and discomfort in basic daily activities like just getting out of bed and getting moving in the morning. I have found a series of arch supports from the Good Feet Store to minimize the discomfort of walking, regular exercise, balance and daily mobility. They consist of three arches that go in my shoes: a trainer arch that is only worn for an hour and feels for that hour like I am walking on golf balls and creates a more balanced feeling in my feet, a maintainer arch system that gives me better balance and mobility during regular daily activities, and a relaxer arch system that is for later in the afternoon and evening.

These arches and regular exercises, provided years ago by a gifted trainer, have helped me maintain my mobility and stay active and lead an extraordinarily mobile life. One of my favorite activities is hiking in the Pacific Northwest, and I enjoy doing this with friends and family.

During the medical tests done at the VA hospital, a doctor noticed that I had a low thyroid result, and so I have been taking medication for this for about nine years. For a number of years, I had a case of jungle foot that was cleared up with medications by our dermatologist.

In my later years, I enjoyed college teaching and I thought how lucky we are to live at this time when there are so many medical procedures and forms of assistance to help prop us up and stay mobile and engaged in productive and satisfying work. Getting ready for the day takes a little bit of time and effort to put oneself together, but the result is that the quality of our lives is enhanced by these inventions and medical advances over the past few years. Of course, my story is a very ordinary one compared to the challenges many people face in their lives.

I am grateful for living at this particular time, for the VA benefits that provided much of my education and additional flight training, and for the professionals who work in the VA medical profession. I look forward to the exciting adventures that may be in my future. I have been blessed with a long and very satisfying life after Vietnam. I often remember the 30 flight crewmembers from our unit and the more than 58,000 men and women whose lives ended in Vietnam and who have not had these additional years.

* * *

When I returned from Vietnam, like others who have been in a combat environment for a year, I had the occasional start from loud noises that would cause me to flinch and feel like jumping under the nearest bed for cover from incoming mortar rounds. While driving a car, it was uncomfortable if people pulled up next to me. I always envisioned getting zapped from the side, where I couldn't see the shooter. I went to a few war movies early on and ended up going up to the ticket window and demanding my money back because I had seen enough of this stuff for real and didn't want to pay for it for entertainment purposes. These are typical and very minor reactions after being in a combat situation.

Probably the most visible forms of annoyance for my family involved the need to walk around the house in the dark at night to check the doors, and a preoccupation with hyper-organizing my environment that came from almost being thrown out of Warrant Officer Candidate School for demerits and disorganization of personal effects.

I remember watching a video about Vietnam veterans and their spouses going through a healing retreat exercise, and one veteran was asked why he felt the need to carry a sidearm when hiking in the mountains. He responded, "There might be some scary people up there."

His wife chimed in, "The only scary person up there carrying a weapon is you!"

As part of the VA intake process, I also met with a psychologist in a glass high-rise building in downtown Seattle who ran me through a number of tests and interview questions, but his conclusion was that I had experienced quite a bit of combat in 1967–68 but that I seemed well adjusted with no typical signs of PTSD.

19

Memories, Legacy, Faith

Over the years, I have been invited to speak on Veterans Day on a number of occasions. I have made these speeches in public and private schools, at the elementary and secondary levels, to school boards and city councils, at a university, in churches, and to civic groups about what Veterans Day means to me. The following is the speech that I have developed and given over the years. I think that these invitations represent a sincere interest on the part of those making the invitation and a unique opportunity to share a perspective from a primary-source participant in the Vietnam War. When I have given these talks, I am always surprised at the unexpected and uniquely personal responses they bring out from those in attendance. I share this with you in the hope that other Vietnam veterans might consider making these talks and sharing their ideas and use any of mine they think might be relevant. I tend to write out what I am going to say and then I study the material and give the talk spontaneously like I am winging it:

Thank you for the invitation to speak on this Veterans Day. I am honored to be your Veterans Day speaker. I give these talks in memory of some very special people who have not had the opportunity to live as I have.

When I was 20 years old I told my friends that I wanted to learn to fly. I started taking flying lessons at Paine Field in Everett, Washington, and the most exciting day in my young life was when I first soloed an airplane. Since I was a teacher during my life I am going to weave some lessons into my talk today. The first lesson is: **Treasure your dreams. You never know where they will take you.**

I enjoyed learning to fly, but it cost a lot of money and I didn't know how I could afford to pursue my dream of learning to fly. One day I saw a poster in a storefront in downtown Seattle that said you could learn to fly helicopters in the Army. I stopped in the place and found out it was an Army recruiting office. They said the Army was looking for young men in good physical condition who were intelligent and interested in learning to fly helicopters. I said that sounded like me. They invited me back to take written test called the FAST test. It stood for Flight Aptitude Standards Test. I took it and passed. They said, "You qualified, and if you want to become an Army helicopter pilot you can enlist for that school and you can enter next week." They also said, "If you become an Army warrant officer and a helicopter pilot after the training you are probably going to go to Vietnam." I thought it over for a day or so and decided I would enlist. My second lesson is: **When opportunity knocks, answer the door.**

I was assigned to Fort Polk, Louisiana, for basic training as an infantry soldier. This training was to prepare me mentally and physically to be a combat soldier. It was tough and I made many friends who supported me and we all learned to support each other. My third lesson is: **Friendships are among life's greatest gifts.**

There were many new and difficult things to learn, and learning implies that you don't know how to do something when you start but if you work hard at it you can learn anything you set your mind to. My fourth lesson is: **Be humble. Realize that learning often means you don't know what you are doing at the start. But stay with it and you can learn new skills and information no matter how hard it seems.**

Sometimes we were pushed very hard to stretch our physical and mental abilities, and some of my friends got discouraged, but the ones who worked hard and stayed with it learned the new skills. My fifth lesson is: **Have a positive attitude. It makes all the difference!**

When I was in flight school it was a lot of study and learning and it was exciting. We learned how to fly first in lessons in a classroom, and then we applied the lessons in learning to fly actual helicopters. The flight instructors would tell us what to do, show us how to do it, and then we would have a chance to try and try again until we learned the skills. It was hard work, and we practiced everything over and over again until doing them was second nature. We even practiced how to land a helicopter if the engine quit. This skill saved my life two times in Vietnam when the helicopter I was flying had an engine failure. My sixth lesson is: **Practice, practice, practice until you really learn something.**

My sixth lesson is: **Study history**. You might ask, "Why?" Because if you study history, you will know why some civilizations thrive and some disappear. Historians have documented that, over history, 22 civilizations have flourished and vanished, and they have identified the main reasons why these civilizations collapsed:

1. They lost their sense of right and wrong.
2. They became obsessed with pleasure for pleasure's sake.
3. They let their money lose its value.
4. Honest work ceased to be a value.
5. Respect for law and order disintegrated and violence became accepted for getting what individuals and groups wanted.

6. They got to a point where the citizens of the country would not fight for the country and so they paid soldiers from other countries to defend them.

So here is lesson number seven: **Always do what's right**

Lesson number eight: **Be willing to put off immediate pleasure for a long-term greater good**

Lesson number nine is: **Learn about the value of your money and use it wisely**

Lesson number 10 is: **Work hard**

Lesson number 11 is: **Respect the law and the rights of others**

My final lesson is number 12: **Value and appreciate the choice that some people make to serve our country in the military.**

Thirty flight crewmembers from my unit gave the ultimate sacrifice of their lives in the Vietnam War. Nine of these men were known to me and gave their lives during the year that I was there. I would like to ask for nine volunteers to help me remember these men by holding a rubbing I have made off the Vietnam Wall in Washington, D.C., of their name and bringing it up and placing it on the table by the American flag as I read them. I will read these names as I read lines of the Pledge of Allegiance to conclude my talk today. Remember to show respect for the flag and our country when the Pledge of Allegiance is recited at a sports game or the start of a program.

I pledge allegiance to the flag—Captain Franklin S. Bradley

Of the United States of America—Warrant Officer Ricky Lee Hull

And to the Republic—Specialist Paul R. Anzelone

For which it stands—Specialist Michael Lynch

One nation–Chief Warrant Officer Francis L. Griffin

Under God—Specialist Michael Edward Eckerfield Indivisible—
Warrant Officer William G. Moncrief

With liberty—Specialist George S. Hadzega

And justice for all—Specialist Willie B. Catling

On behalf of these great men and their ultimate sacrifice I thank you for the privilege of speaking to you today.

After Vietnam, like many of my fellow veterans, I had a deep sense of responsibility to make a difference with the rest of my life. I would like to be remembered for having lived an ordinary life of service and adventure and for always striving to listen, learn, grow, and help improve the quality of life for others.

To my family. I love my wife and family members deeply. I didn't always show it to them in my actions and priorities. They endured my personal quirks in terms of being hyper-organized, intolerant of violence in movies, and goal-oriented to distraction at times in pursuing my goals, dreams, interests, and hobbies.

To my country as a combat helicopter pilot and Army chief warrant officer in Vietnam during the Vietnam War.

To the city of Langley, Washington, as appointed and elected mayor.

To students, staff, and parents in four high-quality public school districts as a teacher and administrator.

To two high-quality Catholic schools, the students, staff, parents and patrons, as a teacher and administrator.

To the Catholic Youth Organization (CYO) camping program, staff and campers as a camper, counselor, and director.

To my beloved Catholic Church as a parish council president, Catholic school principal, Eucharistic minister, director of stewardship, second degree Knight of Columbus, musician, and CCD teacher.

To my fellow veterans through the Whidbey Veterans Resource Center as interim VRC director and WVRC development advisor.

To my siblings as a proud brother and the executor of my parents' estate.

To my profession in publishing two educational books on employee recognition and a memoir of my Vietnam experience.

To the WWU Administration Certification Program and graduate students by teaching principal and superintendent applicants part-time and mentoring graduates for eight years in the Woodring College of Education.

To the communities I have worked in on various ad hoc committees and task forces.

To my friends in sharing the joy of various activities and adventures with family, special friends and strangers in flying, sailing, hiking, motorcycle riding, old vehicle restoration, fishing, camping, writing, guitar playing, song writing, singing and public speaking and presenting.

To our neighbors in living our lives and being a helpful neighbor in Seattle at our condo by the Locks, on Whidbey Island in Langley, in Bellingham at our condo, and in Mount Baker at our log cabin, and many years in Marysville.

I have been an active Catholic for my whole life and attribute my ability to process my Vietnam experience and move on from it into a productive life afterwards to my faith and belief system. I believe in the fundamental precepts of my Church but not all of the formal positions it takes. I also believe that the highest form of moral judgment comes from an informed conscience. I feel responsible to use my talents, skills, and abilities to improve the quality of life for others. I developed some leadership abilities in combat in Vietnam that have been the basis for a life of leadership and responsibility in education, public service, in the communities I have served, and in my church. I believe our lives consist of a temporal life on this earth and an eternal life afterwards.

Reflected in my writing, poems, stories, and letters home is a sense of personal responsibility for my actions, compassion for others, forgiveness of myself and others, and hope that the Vietnam War had some positive implications for improving the quality of life for others. I realize that some considered the Vietnam War a dark part of our nation's history, and others felt it was a war with no positive outcomes. I don't share those points of view. I knew many courageous people for whom I have the greatest respect and admiration who served in the military during Vietnam. We did the best we could as soldiers and aviators with the information and assignments we had at the time.

We had a Catholic chaplain on our airbase in Vietnam, and he conducted regular masses and the sacraments for us and memorials when someone was killed in action. As I recall, he also served the other bases in the Delta. There was a chapel on our airfield that was a place to go to reflect and consider the responsibilities we were carrying out in our assigned missions each day. He flew in helicopters in the unit on missions with some of the pilots. His presence was an important part of the operation of our base. I believed in the noble causes we were fighting for in supporting American values of freedom and democracy and resisting communism and oppression. History will ultimately judge our efforts.

20

Reunions and Memorials

In the half-century since I was a helicopter pilot in Vietnam, I have enjoyed belonging to two Vietnam-related flight crew organizations. The first is the 121st Aviation Association and the second is the Vietnam Helicopter Pilots Association (VHPA).

The VHPA includes any pilot from any military service who flew helicopters as their primary assignment in Vietnam. This organization has an annual reunion in a city in the United States and it is a large conference. I have attended a few of these reunions and remember one in particular, the 30-year reunion in San Francisco, where our whole family attended and enjoyed seeing the other families and pilots as well.

The 121st Aviation Association also has an annual conference in a strategic location, and it is much smaller group because it includes the officers and enlisted personnel from the units that were stationed at Soc Trang associated with the 121st Assault Helicopter Company.

A Date with an Old Girlfriend UH1B 64–13972

A friend of mine, Bob Bogash, has been instrumental in putting teams of what he calls "ghosts" together to acquire and restore iconic aircraft for the Seattle Museum of Flight. The "ghosts" are pilots, mechanics, philanthropists, enthusiasts, flight crewmembers, and uniquely skilled experts. His motto is "Go big or go home!" Among the aircraft he and his teams have acquired are the first Boeing 727, a British/French Concorde, the "Midnight Express" Vietnam B-52, and a Constellation. He believes (on a stack of Bibles) that aircraft have "souls" and can speak to "ghosts."

I was a CW2 fire team leader in UH-1B gunships with the 121st Assault Helicopter Company stationed at Soc Trang, RVN, from December 1967 to December 1968. We were in "The World Famous Soc Trang Tigers." Humility was not considered a virtue in our company. My call sign was Viking 23. A fellow pilot in the 121st, Tom Jameson, texted me and said, "Hey padre,

The Viking logo was on the nose cone of each of the gunships of the 121st Assault Helicopter Company. Our company had many colorful nose cone art examples that are among the best examples of this art form from the Vietnam War. Most were the work of an anonymous but highly skilled painter from the nearby town of Soc Trang. In the gunship platoon our ships all had this logo of a Viking with rockets under his arms and M60 machine guns in his hands blasting away. Hanoi Hannah picked up on this logo and the fear it instilled in the enemy by calling us over the radio airwaves "the Blue Diamond Devils of the Delta" (Shannon McCarthy).

My family members and I thought we would take a few selfies and then be on our way after spending some time with the aircraft, but the lovely ladies in the public relations department at Fort Jackson, unbeknown to us, had contacted the local news media and we were greeted by three TV news teams and two radio news teams from Columbia, South Carolina. This picture of me is a favorite of mine in that it captures not only the spiritual connection but also the physical connection that a pilot makes with an aircraft that has been flown on some memorable missions and brought the crew home (photograph by Shannon McCarthy).

did you know that the aircraft you commanded made it back from our unit in Vietnam and is on display in South Carolina at Fort Jackson?"

My older son, Michael, a businessman and regional supervisor for Springfree Trampolines, does business in Texas and Georgia and loves visiting historic Charleston, South Carolina. He invited his mother and me to accompany his family there on an epic four-day vacation just before Christmas 2019. I didn't want to hijack the trip over an old girlfriend, but since I had found out that Fort Jackson was only a two-hour drive away, I thought, "What the hell!!

Why don't we add a little romantic side trip?" I found a picture of the "old girl" on Google Maps using a website titled "Tour of Honor." It is a list, data, and coordinates of all displayed Vietnam helicopters. I made a few calls to the fort's public information office, and was tickled with their enthusiasm for facilitating such a reunion.

Our visit occurred on December 23, 2019. There was a monsoon rain falling over South Carolina, the wind was howling, and there was a powerful storm front in the whole area. I brought my old Class A uniform I hadn't worn in 50 years, my treasured Viking beret, a black Viking T-shirt we wore back then, and my tail rotor chain wristband, and wore my flight school class ring to be dressed appropriately for the reunion pictures we planned to take with our cell phones. Four ladies from the public information office at Fort Jackson went out of their way to welcome us to the base. Their names were Veran, Darcie, Julie, and Leslie.

Our arrival was deferred by a car fire on the interstate highway. As we were delayed a few minutes in traffic on approach, we notified our hosts, who mentioned that the three TV news teams and two radio station reporters were waiting. This of course was quite an unexpected surprise, and I was glad I had written out and rehearsed a few thoughts ahead of time. My family said, "Hey, this is more than we expected!"

"Papa, are you going to introduce us?"

"Yes, of course!"

My granddaughter Lizah, eight years old, piped up, "Tell them I like animals!"

"OK, I'll tell them you sing in the Seattle Girls Choir, and if I get a chance I'll mention you like animals."

We arrived at Gate #2 and were escorted by LA to the museum, passing the aircraft with its distinctive Viking logo in a menacing raked climb out attitude perched in a fitting display for the old girl from Vietnam. I was breathless at seeing her restored in all her splendid glory but noticed right away that she was not wearing a few of the defining attributes I remembered her for. The 2.75 rocket pods on each side and the mini guns were missing, as were the call sign and cherries logo on the doors.

We stepped into the high-quality museum and I disappeared into the restroom to transform from retired educator and politician to warrant officer. When I emerged they put three microphones on me and we took off. The brief talk and interview went very well. I looked over some printed memorabilia they had spread out like photographs after Vietnam, an original checklist, and data sheets they had for the aircraft, and then we adjourned to look at her in the pouring rain and take some more pictures.

The millennial-aged news crews were real troopers despite the rains and made me feel important by asking for individual selfies with me afterwards. I thought to myself, "Boy, we never got this response when we came back from Nam." A young Marine Corps vet called me "sir," smiled, and said he was deeply honored to meet me. I told everyone how impressive the display was.

I remember at least one song written in the sixties about meeting up with an old girlfriend and realizing the magic wasn't there anymore. Well, for the benefit of my former fellow gun drivers in the Vikings, I can truly say, she looked even better than ever with age. And you too should go down and see her.

Our unit has at least one other display, a Vietnam helicopter gunship survivor that is at a memorial site in Angel Fire, New Mexico. It was flown on a memorable Easter Sunday mission in 1967 as a smoke ship by Father Jerry Daly, then Chief Warrant Officer Daly, one of the most decorated helicopter pilots in the Vietnam War, and our version of World War II's Pappy Boyington of the Black Sheep Squadron. After he made 13 runs and laid down smoke to cover saving the survivors of multiple crews who were shot down in the landing zone, the ship was so full of bullet holes it had to be taken out of service, "red Xed" as we used to say.

I was very fortunate to be in a company with this kind of history and this kind of men. We were berated by Hanoi Hannah over the airwaves out of radio North Vietnam as those "Blue Diamond Devils of the Delta." I can't think of a more exciting and fitting tribute to a bunch of young 20-something helicopter pilots from the Vietnam War.

Interspersed with the Pledge of Allegiance I read the names of nine of our friends who were lost as flight crewmembers in 1968, out of the 30 total who gave their lives for their friends and the mission from the Tigers and Vikings with our unit during the war. We must never forget them. I do believe that UH-1B 64–13972 has a "soul," and I am so honored to have earned the title of a "ghost" from my friend Bob.

The last interview question was the most difficult to answer: "Did this helicopter have a name when you flew her?"

"Yes," I responded. "Yes, but it was sort of politically incorrect and a surprise that my crew chief thought up and told me about later after he had already painted it on. It probably became one of the most well-known helicopters by its name in our unit and in the IV Corps area of the Mekong Delta. Are you sure you want to know?"

"Of course we do!" replied the news crews.

"Well," I said, hesitating a moment: "It was called the Cherry Buster, and it had two big red cherries and Viking 23 painted on each door!"

I notice they are not there now and that's OK. Those of us who know her know her name. All I can say is we were soldiers once and we were so young. We were "Above the Best." The best were down in the jungles and rice paddies, and we did everything we could to support them. We are all proud of being Vietnam veterans and helicopter flight crewmembers. For many of us it changed our lives forever.

This monument to 5,000 helicopter pilots and flight crewmembers who made the ultimate sacrifice for the mission and in support of the ground troops from 1961 to 1975 in Vietnam did not just happen. It was because of the efforts of Mr. Bob Hesslebein and a dedicated Legacy Committee of VHPA volunteers over a number of years and through many channels and exceptions to standard rules and regulations that this monument exists where it should be in Arlington National Cemetery for generations to see and remember (Lisa Kirk McAndrew; courtesy *VHPA Aviator*).

Arlington National Cemetery is the nation's preeminent memorial to those who have made the ultimate sacrifice for our country. The helicopters flying overhead in a V "missing man" formation with one helicopter missing reminds us that there was a significant cost in terms of human life during and after this war, as there is in all wars. Missing for many who returned from combat in Vietnam was the thanks of a grateful nation. Our country learned a lesson from Vietnam. The soldiers who fought there did the best they could and in some cases felt blamed for the war. Today there is a better understanding of the costs incurred in waging a war and the country regularly expresses gratitude for the men and women who are willing to put themselves in harm's way to serve honorably this country that we love. Identity of individuals unknown (Carolyn Kirk; courtesy *VHPA Aviator*).

Monuments and Memorials

Soc Trang Tigers and Vikings Monument, Fort Rucker, Alabama

In the summer of 2012, my wife, Shannon, and I returned to the Army Helicopter Training Center at Fort Rucker, Alabama, for a very special dedication. Members from our company, the 121st Assault Helicopter Company, that were stationed at Soc Trang and also at Da Nang, came from all across the country to dedicate a beautiful black marble monument to 30 flight crewmembers who made the ultimate sacrifice during their tour of duty during the time our unit was actively involved in the Vietnam War.

A procession occurred during the dedication ceremony that involved the laying of a memorial wreath. Memorials remember the dead but express the feelings of the living. The pilots, flight crewmembers, dignitaries, Gold Star families, members of the VHPA, ministers, musicians, Vietnam veterans and grateful patriotic citizens shared a solemn moment as the wreath representing the thousands was placed during the monument dedication. Identity of individuals unknown (Lisa Kirk McAndrew; courtesy *VHPA Aviator*).

It is fitting that a simple granite monument with the picture of a Huey helicopter, the dates of the Vietnam War, and the symbols of the services of our
country would be the headstone for these brave flight crewmembers. They
were courageous in battle, dedicated and willing to lay down their lives for the
mission, their fellow soldiers, and their friends. No greater love than this can
there be. Military service has been one of those pillars that represent a strong
nation going back in history to the earliest of times and conflicts. The crowd
that assembled for this memorable day was a cross section of America here to
honor the legacy of these brave flight crewmembers. The commanding officer
of our company in Vietnam was Colonel Carl McNair. He was our leader during
the 1968 Tet Offensive of the 121st Assault Helicopter Company, "The World
Famous Soc Trang Tigers," and he returned to give the keynote speech at this
dedication. Attendees at the Monument Dedication, left to right: Retired Colonel Herrick and Retired Brigadier General Carl McNair (Lisa Kirk McAndrew;
courtesy *VHPA Aviator*).

Vietnam Helicopter Pilots and Crewmembers Monument in Arlington National Cemetery, Washington, D.C.

On April 18, 2018, after years of dedicated hard work and advocacy on the part of leaders of the Vietnam Helicopter Pilots Association, a very

These retired high-ranking Army officers who attended the memorial dedication were in charge of infantry and aviation units in Vietnam. There was a special bond between the soldiers in the jungles and rice paddies and the flight crews that brought them in, covered them, and pulled them out of combat. As flight crewmembers we were reminded we were "Above the Best." That meant we were flying above the best. The best were down in the jungles and rice paddies, and we needed to do everything we could to help and support them. The Vietnam Wall is a sacred monument that has a special meaning for veterans. This monument, a short distance away in this special place, will be a sacred reminder far into the future of the Vietnam War and the sacrifices made by so many. The friendships forged in a combat situation are among the most endearing of life's relationships. We will always remember the ultimate sacrifice made by so many. Left to right: Major Frank Moreno, Colonel Paul Winkel, Colonel Bob St. Louis, Brigadier General Jack Nicholson (Col. Robert St. Louis; courtesy *VHPA Aviator*).

special monument was placed in Arlington National Cemetery to commemorate forever the lives of 5,000 flight crewmembers who were lost during the Vietnam War. A featured speaker at the dedication was Brigadier General Carl McNair, who was our company commander in 1968. Father Jerry Daly, who was the Vikings platoon leader for our gunship platoon in 1967–1968, gave the benediction.

How fitting it was for Bob Hesselbein (left), past VHPA president and chairman of the VHPA Legacy Committee, to introduce Father Jerry Daly, former Viking platoon leader and Catholic priest, to lead the gathered in a benediction of this sacred monument: two warriors returning in their civilian roles to honor those who made the ultimate sacrifice for their country (Lisa Kirk McAndrew; courtesy *VHPA Aviator*).

A Headstone for Thousands: A Long Journey Completed by Tom Kirk

For many, the Vietnam Helicopter Pilots and Crewmembers Monument seemed like a unicorn—many details but no sightings.

The VHPA envisioned a non-governmental funded, logical, appropriate and well-deserved symbol for the men who left our ranks while flying in the "Helicopter War." Bob Hesselbein was appointed chairman of the Legacy Committee and immediately entered a world where logic (if used) was skewed. Due to his efforts, the support of the members of our organization, some legislative benefactors, and officials supportive of the project, all of the challenges were overcome. The long-awaited monument was dedicated on April 18, 2018, with suitable ceremony and in the presence of several thousand people.

I attended as a member of the Legacy Committee, not a reporter. The print and electronic coverage has been widespread and comprehensive as well as available well in advance of this issue's printing. I can add, however, what the cameras may not have revealed. Many in the audience honoring our fallen brothers were Gold Star Family members, friends, currently serving members of our Armed Forces, and even a contingent of VNAF pilots. The emotions they displayed were as varied as their status.

There are too many names to list as participants on this long journey to that sunny April day. I hope those who went before us had a "sky box" for the event.

Appendix: The Men Who Gave Their Lives

The 30 men from the 121st Assault Helicopter Company who gave their lives for the mission and their friends during the Vietnam War

Anderson	David B.	SP4	5-Apr-69
Anzelone	Paul R.	SP5	9-Feb-68
Aydlett	James Quinel	1st Lt	11-Jul-66
Bradley, Jr.	Franklin S.	CPT	9-Feb-68
Braman	Donald L.	SP4	2-Jan-63
Carson	Chad Leonard	SGT	10-Dec-69
Catling	Willie B.	SP4	2-Jul-68
Christmas	Loye T.	PFC	17-Jan-64
Coffman	Clyde L.	SP5	2-Apr-70
Eckerfield	Michael David	SP5	26-Sep-68
Fitts	Charles Milton	1st LT	11-Jan-63
Fox	Lorenzo	SP4	31-Aug-70
Griffin	Francis Lekirklas	CW-2	1-Feb-68
Hadzega	George S.	SP4	15-Jun-68
Hargrove	James W.	CW-2	18-Oct-66
Hull	Ricky Lee	WO-1	9-Feb-68
Jones	Jackie Dallas	WO-1	11-Jul-66
Kreis	Sherwood David	WO-1	29-Sep-69
Lynch	Michael	SP4	9-Feb-68
Moncrief	William Grady	WO-1	3-Jul-68
Nance	David E.	PFC	11-Jul-66
Sferrazza	Angelo J.	SP4	11-Jul-66

Silva	Thomas J.	SP4	3-Apr-70
Smith	Philip Edwin, Jr.	SP4	17-Jan-70
Snyder	Preston J.	SP4	18-May-66
Stone	Lewis Lynn	1st LT	11-Jan-63
Toth	Donald Bonney	CPT	11-Jan-63
Umbenhauer	Dale E.	PFC	17-May-66
Vaspory	William L.	SGT	2-Apr-70
Warden	Richard John	WO-1	4-Jul-70

Author's Service History

CW2 Frederick C. McCarthy (5 years total), U.S. Army

Basic and Advanced Infantry Training—Fort Polk, Louisiana
Dec 1966–Mar 1967
Primary Helicopter Flight Training—Fort Wolters, Texas
Mar 1967–Jul 1967
Advanced Helicopter Flight Training—Fort Rucker, Alabama
Aug 1967–Dec 1967
Warrant Officer–Helicopter Pilot—121st Assault Helicopter
Company—Soc Trang, Vietnam Dec 1967–Dec 1968
Meteorology and Flight Subjects Instructor—Fort Wolters, Texas
Jan 1969–Dec 1969
Pilot–540th Assault Helicopter Company–WA State National
Guard—Fort Lewis, Washington Oct 1970–Jun 1971
Pilot–92nd Avn Co—U.S. Army Reserve—Paine Airfield, Everett,
Washington—Dec 1975–Sep 1977

Awards and Decorations—DD 214

National Defense Service Medal
Army Aviator Badge
Vietnam Service Medal
Vietnam Campaign Medal
Air Medal with Two Oakleaf Clusters with "V" device
Air Medal Meritorious Service
Two Overseas Bars

Miscellaneous Data

1,300 flight hours of
    helicopter missions
    in Vietnam
UH-1 D & H model
    slicks and UH-1B
    model gunships
Tet Offensive of 1968
Soc Trang Tigers and
    Vikings

Helicopters

Hughes TH 55
Bell TH 47
UH-1 A, B, D, H
    Hueys
Sikorsky CH 34
Hiller OH 23

Class A uniform after Vietnam tour. In this photograph, I see the experience of 1,300 flight hours of missions, surviving the war, and what being in combat does to age a young person. At the time, I wrote to my parents that I was 22 but felt like I was 42.

Bibliography

Babbs, Ken. *Who Shot the Water Buffalo?* New York: Overlook Press, 2011.

Ballentine, David A. *Gunbird Driver.* Annapolis, MD: Naval Institute Press, 2008.

Batecchi, Carl E., M.D. *Soc Trang: A Vietnamese Odyssey.* Boulder, CO: Rocky Mountain Writers Guild, 1980.

Beaver, Victor. *The Sky Soldiers.* West Conshohocken, PA: Infinity, 2001, 2004.

Brokaw, Thomas. *The Greatest Generation.* New York: Random House, 1998, 2004.

Burns, Ken, and Lynn Novick. *The Vietnam War.* Washington, D.C.: PBS Film Series, 2018.

Carlock, Chuck. *Firebirds.* Arlington, TX: Summit Publishing Group, 1995.

Corley, David Lee. *A War Too Far.* Telos LLC, 2019.

Dandridge, W. Larry. *Blades of Thunder.* Charleston, SC: Tigers, Vikings, and Vipers Publishing LLC, 2015.

Eastman, David L. *Outlaws in Vietnam.* Portsmouth, NH: Peter E. Randall Publisher, 2001.

Hackworth, David. *About Face: The Odyssey of an American Warrior.* New York: Touchstone, 1989.

_____. *Steel My Soldiers' Hearts.* New York: Rugged Land LLC, 2002.

Hoyland, Jay. *Through the Eyes of the Tiger.* New York: iUniverse, Inc, 2009.

Kalista, C.J. *Military Products Reference Data.* Fort Worth, TX: Bell Helicopter, 1967.

Logevall, Fredrik. *Embers of War: The Fall of an Empire, and the Making of America's Vietnam.* New York: Penguin Random House, 2012.

Marlantes, Karl. *Matterhorn.* New York: Grove Press, 2010.

_____. *What It Is Like to Go to War.* New York: Grove Press, 2011.

Marshall, Tom. *The Price of Exit.* New York: Ballantine Books, 1998.

McClellan, Orrin. *A Soldier's Journal: Last Supper to No Goodbye.* Soap Lake, WA: Gorman McClellan Resources, LLC, 2018.

McGhee, Col. John Gillespie, Jr. Poem "High Flight," U.S. Air Force, 1941.

Mutza, Wayne. *U.S. Army Aviation in Vietnam.* Carrollton, TX: Squadron/Signal Publications, 2009.

Piotrowski, Pete. *Basic Airman to General: The Secret War & Other Conflicts: Lessons in Leadership & Life.* Xlibris Corporation, 2014.

Reeder, William, Jr. *Through the Valley.* Annapolis, MD: Naval Institute Press, 2016.

Rowe, James N. *Five Years to Freedom.* New York: Ballantine Books, 1971.

Spaulding, Richard D. *Centaur Flights.* New York: Ballantine Books, 1997.

Vermillion, Steve. *Dustoff.* Puyallup, WA: Wild 'n' Woolly Publishing, 2003.

Walzer, Michael. *Just and Unjust Wars.* New York: Basic Books, 2015.

Index